STATE V. O'NEILL

Sixth Edition

State v. O'Neill

Sixth Edition

James H. Seckinger

Professor of Law
University of Notre Dame Law School

Maureen A. Howard

Associate Professor of Law
Director of Trial Advocacy
University of Washington School of Law

NATIONAL INSTITUTE FOR TRIAL ADVOCACY

Address inquiries to:

Reprint Permission
National Institute for Trial Advocacy
1685 38th Street, Suite 200
Boulder, CO 80301-2735
Phone: (800) 225-6482
Fax: (720) 890-7069
E-mail: permissions@nita.org

ISBN 978-1-60156-208-1
FBA 1208

14 13 12 11 10 9 8 7 6 5 4 3 2 1
Printed in the United States of America

CONTENTS

INTRODUCTION

Defendent view

The Grand Jury has charged Joseph J. O'Neill with first degree murder of his estranged wife, Liza Wilson O'Neill, on September 10, YR-1.

Did he go somewhere else?

The State alleges that the defendant, Joseph J. O'Neill, shot and killed his wife on the front porch of her stepmother's house at 1704 East Prospect Street in Nita City. An eyewitness, the deceased's stepmother, claims she saw the defendant drive up in his car along the curb in front of the house and fire a gun that struck and killed Liza Wilson O'Neill. The shooting occurred at approximately 10:00 p.m. It was dark and raining. → *vision impeded (were there lights?)*

what car was it?

what was he doing

The defendant Joseph J. O'Neill has pleaded not guilty. He vigorously asserts his innocence and claims he was elsewhere at the time of his wife's death.

The case went to trial and ended in a hung jury. The State has elected to pursue the charges against Mr. O'Neill and to take the case to trial again. The testimony of the defendant, Joseph J. O'Neill, from the first trial may not be used by the State during its case-in-chief, but may be used for impeachment if the defendant elects to take the stand at the second trial. → *Do not let 1st witness statement?*

The applicable law is contained in the statutes and proposed jury instructions that are set forth at the end of the case file.

All years in these materials are stated in the following form:

YR-0   indicates the actual year in which the case is being tried (the present year);

YR-1   indicates the next preceding year (use the actual year;

YR-2   indicates the second preceding year (please use the actual year), etc.

SPECIAL INSTRUCTIONS FOR USE AS A FULL TRIAL

When this case file is used as a basis for a full trial, the following witnesses may be called by the parties:

State:
- Mrs. Mary Wilson
- Officer Frank Novak
- Ms. Maria Vargas

Defendant:
Mr. Joseph J. O'Neill

Ms. Amber Donovan

Ms. Sam Russo

Optional witness for either side: Sergeant John Pierce

[In lieu of calling Pierce as a witness, either party may read his report into evidence. See Stipulations, below.]

A party need not call all of the listed witnesses. Any or all of the witnesses can be called by either party, except that the state may not call the defendant as a witness. However, if a witness is to be called by a party other than the one for whom he or she is listed, the party for whom the witness is listed will select and prepare the witness.

STIPULATIONS

The parties are required to enter into the following stipulations:

1. The Coroner's Report was made by the Coroner pursuant to her official duties, and the Report is an official record of Nita County, Nita.

2. The gunshot residue test on Joseph J. O'Neill was performed properly and in accordance with accepted scientific procedures.

3. The admissibility of Sergeant John Pierce's report is stipulated. It may be read to the jury by either party. This stipulation is superseded if any party elects to call Sergeant Pierce as a witness.

4. The defendant moved to suppress statements made to Officer Novak in O'Neill's apartment and en route to the police station as well as his statement made at the police station. He also moved to suppress the gun and the jacket. These motions were fully briefed and argued by counsel, and then denied by the court.

5. The Nita Police Forensic Crime Lab confirmed that an email recovered by the police on Liza O'Neill's laptop, sent from gamerpro_X@gmail.com on September 9, YR-1, originated at the IP address assigned to Amber Donovan's house, where the defendant was living. The lab also examined the defendant's laptop, recovered from his room at Ms. Donovan's house, and confirmed that the email had, in fact, been sent from that laptop.

IN THE CIRCUIT COURT OF NITA COUNTY, NITA

THE PEOPLE OF THE STATE OF NITA	)	
	)	Case No. CR 2126
v.	)	
	)	INDICTMENT
JOSEPH J. O'NEILL,	)	
	)	
Defendant.	)	

The Grand Jury in and for the County of Nita, State of Nita, upon their oath and in the name and by the authority of the State of Nita, does hereby charge the following offense under the Criminal Code of the State of Nita:

That on September 10, YR-1, at and within the County of Nita in the State of NITA, Joseph J. O'Neill committed the crime of

MURDER IN THE FIRST DEGREE

in violation of Section 18-3-102 of the Nita Criminal Code of 1998, as amended, in that he, after deliberation and with the intent to cause the death of Liza Wilson O'Neill or another person, with a deadly weapon, namely a gun, fired said gun and killed the deceased.

Contrary to the form of the Statute and against the peace and dignity of the People of the State of Nita.

A TRUE BILL:

Matthew James

Foreperson of the Grand Jury

Christopher M. Schafbuch

District Attorney

NITA COUNTY

State of Nita, NSBA # 121988

TESTIMONY OF MARY WILSON AT FIRST TRIAL
DECEMBER 15, YR-1

MARY WILSON, called to testify as a witness for the State and having been duly sworn, testified as follows:

1   My name is Mary Wilson. I live at 1704 East Prospect Street, Nita City, Nita. I am fifty-four
2   years old. I am a widow. My husband, John Wilson, died on October 1, YR-12. We had no
3   children. I married him in YR-20. It was my first marriage and his second. His first wife died
4   in YR-22. They had one child, Liza, who was six years old when I married him. Liza was my
5   stepdaughter. John had been a prominent lawyer in Nita City and then, during the first year
6   we were married, he was appointed as a Circuit Court Judge here in Nita City. He was a judge
7   until he died.
8

9   When I married John, he owned the house at 1704 East Prospect. I have lived there ever
10   since. Liza, my stepdaughter, lived there too until she married J.J.—that's Joseph J. O'Neill. In
11   his will, my husband left all his property to me for my life, and then to Liza when I die. The will
12   also set up a trust fund for Liza and me, with the Nita National Bank and Trust Company as
13   trustee. I was also named as Liza's guardian until she turned twenty-one. Her father's estate
14   gives me an income of $80,000 a year on the average, mainly from stocks, bonds, and other
15   investments. The house has been fully paid for since YR-5, so I no longer have a mortgage.
16

17   Liza and I lived comfortably on Prospect Street. Although I never formally adopted her,
18   I always considered her as my very own daughter. I loved her and took care of her upbringing
19   as if she were my own little girl. She was so young, only two, when her own mother died that
20   she could hardly remember her. She called me "mom," and our relationship was always the
21   intimate relationship of mother and daughter. I was interested in her welfare and in her future
22   happiness and always wanted to advise her as her mother.
23

24   I supported Liza, sent her to school, and raised her. For high school, she went to Lakeside, a
25   private boarding school for girls in Tacoma City, Nita. She graduated in YR-8, and continued
26   her education at her father's alma mater, Nita University, where she studied communications.
27   After graduating, she came back to Nita City and got a job working at the Bates Fund. At the *60,000 per year*
28   time of her death she was one of several personal assistants to Gill Bates, the President, and
29   was making about $4,000 a month. She was also getting about $1,000 a month from the trust
30   fund. She lived at home with me before her marriage. I never charged her rent and never
31   asked her to contribute to the maintenance of the house. I know I could have, but I didn't
32   want to—she was my daughter.
33

34   Late in YR-3, she began to date Joseph J. O'Neill. She brought him home one night and
35   introduced him to me as "Joey," but he corrected her and told me he had changed his name *reliant on Liza*
36   to J.J. for "work." When I asked him what he did for a living, he said he was a professional
37   "gamer" and that he had started a business conceptualizing and designing video games. He
38   hadn't sold any of his games, but he believed that his business was poised to take off soon.

1   I asked him what kind of "games" he was talking about, and he said they were virtual urban
2   warfare games where players join a "gang" and played in real time online with other players.
3   He also told me that he was working part-time at a local computer store. Liza always called
4   him Joey, even after he changed his name to J.J. When he and Liza first started dating he was
5   renting a room from his friend's sister. The house was not very fancy. It was just off of Aurora
6   Avenue, up near Northgate.
7
8   From the start, I was skeptical about him—he seemed like such a loser. Not to mention that
9   he seemed too old for Liza. At the time she was just out of college and ready to start her life.
10 Here was this man who had spent time in the army and then never gotten his life together.
11 I never approved of him and as Liza continued to date him, I disliked him even more. I never
12 thought he would make Liza happy, and I warned her against marrying him. I thought it was
13 my duty to her as her mother. I told her I thought he was lazy and shiftless and would ruin her
14 life. I told her she should date other men and that she would find she could do better. As it
15 has turned out my judgment about him was right.

Liza gave J.J money / pitied him

16
17 In the winter and spring of YR-3, J.J. came to our house many times. He and Liza went out
18 three or four times a week. She told me that she had to pay for gas for the car and for the
19 dinners, concerts, and movies they went to because "Joey was short of money." I guess she
20 sort of pitied him.
21
22 In spite of all I did to prevent it, Liza told me in the summer of YR-2 that she was going to
23 marry J.J. I wondered how he expected to support a family. From what I saw he was going to
24 live on her money. I told her many times I didn't think J.J. was the man for her and that her
25 own father and mother, if they were alive, wouldn't approve of this marriage. The more I got
26 to know him, the more I disliked J.J. From what I saw of him while he was dating Liza, I thought
27 he was a lazy good-for-nothing. I admit I never had much use for video games or people who
28 played them, and I particularly hated the fact that J.J. was glamorizing gang violence in the
29 games he was making. I was convinced that he'd break her heart. I thought it was my duty to
30 warn her, as her own mother would have, that this man would never make her happy. I said he
31 was lazy and was just after what little money she had or could expect to have. But she became
32 defiant and said she was almost thirty and they would be married, no matter what I or anyone
33 else said. She said she loved him. This was by far the worst disagreement we ever had. I was
34 heartbroken. I would have done anything to prevent the marriage. If only I had, she would be
35 alive today. But they went ahead and were married by a judge in Nita City on November 15,
36 YR-2. I did not go to the wedding, because I was ill. I did not want to do anything to suggest
37 that I approved of what they were doing, so I sent no wedding gift.
38
39 After their marriage, J.J. and Liza lived in an apartment at 250 Valley Street. Liza continued
40 to work for Mr. Bates, but J.J. quit his job at the computer store so he could stay home and
41 devote all his time to building his video gaming business. Liza was supporting them both.
42 That's exactly what I thought would happen.
43
44 After their wedding, J.J. and Liza would come over to my house a couple times a month.
45 I was always civil toward him even though he admitted he was not making any money from

1   his business. They used to come in his old, black, beat-up Honda Civic. I don't know why Liza

2   didn't buy a new car. She had money. In any case, J.J. always parked the car at the curb right

3   out in front of the house. I had seen it there many times before the night he shot Liza.

4

5   Sometime in late July YR-1, Liza came home one night in a taxi. She had left J.J. after a bitter

6   argument. She said she had tried to get him to give up his gaming and get a full-time job, but

7   that he had refused. I told her I was glad to have her back home without J.J. and that she

8   certainly could live with me.

9

10   After they separated Liza lived with me, and J.J. went back to living with his old roommates.

11   He would come to the house about twice a week and argue with Liza. He wanted her to come

12   back to him. She always refused to unless he quit his gaming and got a "real" job. I never left

13   the house when J.J. came over. I didn't trust him. I was afraid he would do something violent

14   to Liza, and I was also afraid that with all his smooth talk he would get her to go back. After

15   all, it was my house and it was my duty to watch out for her welfare as her mother. I didn't

16   want to see her heart broken any more than it was already. I told her not to go back to him

17   and urged her to consider divorcing him.

18

19   Several times, I told J.J. in very plain language what I—as Liza's mother—thought of it all.

20   I told him he was lazy and a deadbeat to be living off his wife's income. He and I argued

21   several times in front of Liza, and a couple of times he threatened me. He said something

22   about getting even with me because I had broken up his marriage to Liza. I am not sure of his

23   exact words, but that's what he meant. And several times he threatened to hurt me or Liza

24   for ruining his marriage. This man had a violent temper. Sometimes he would try to coax Liza

25   to come back to him. Other times he would fly into a rage.

26

27   One time in late August, YR-1, he was at the house arguing with Liza and got angry and rushed

28   out. He slammed the front door so hard I thought he broke it. I ran to the door and opened

29   it and saw him run down the walk. I saw him get into his car at the curb across the street.

30   I could see him clearly, even though it was about 9:30 p.m. and dark and raining. I watched

31   him get into the car, and then, before he drove away, I saw him lean out of the car window

32   and give me the finger. I was standing at the door, and I could easily see him and recognize his

33   face—pale and sort of drawn.

34

35   As I said, he had an uncontrollable temper. When he came to see Liza, he would shout and

36   scream and say that she was "heartless" and "selfish," and he'd turn on me and accuse me of

37   breaking up his marriage. A couple of times he swore and cursed at us. Then he'd storm out

38   of the house, but a few days later he'd be back, and the same things would happen again. Liza

39   would never leave the house with him. He would ask her to go with him "to talk things over"

40   where I couldn't be around. She would never do it; she told me she was afraid of him. When

41   she said that, I told her to never, ever leave the house with him. I was really afraid that he

42   would do some violence to her.

43

44   The last time he visited her before he killed her was on September 9, YR-1. I was present. He

45   didn't fight with her then, and he only stayed for about an hour—from about 9:00 to 10:00 p.m.

1   He asked her to come back to him. He said, "Liza, I'm asking you for the last time. You'd better
2   listen to me now or there are totally going to be consequences." And she said, "Joey, I'm not
3   coming back until you get a real job and give up on this ridiculous video game stuff." He said,
4   "You know I won't do that. I'm not giving up my work, even for you." She said, "Then this is the
5   way it's got to be. I'm done, Joey. I'm sorry it worked out like this." Then J.J. said, "Well, I guess
6   there's no use trying anymore, the way you feel. I won't bother you again. But don't forget
7   this—you're going to regret what you've done to me." Then he screamed at me, "You evil, bitter
8   old woman! You did this! I hate you! You turned Liza against me. You broke up this marriage,
9   and I won't forget that. Whatever happens now is on you!" I cannot swear to the exact words
10 used that night, but I do remember the substance of what each said. He left the house at about
11 10:00 p.m.

13 The next day, September 10, was Liza's birthday. We had dinner at 6:00 p.m., and I gave her a
14 ring for a present. At about 7:00 p.m., she left the house to go to a movie at the Harvard Exit
15 Theater. She said she would be home around 10:00 p.m. She went alone. The theater is on
16 East Roy Street, about fifteen blocks away, and she walked. It wasn't raining then, but it was
17 supposed to so she took an umbrella with her. It was a warm sort of fall evening. After she
18 left I went upstairs. I noticed that she had left the lights on in her room—the front bedroom
19 on the east side of the house. I went in to turn them off, and I noticed she had left her front
20 door key and her cell phone on the night table. I also saw her laptop was open and her e-mail
21 was still up. I closed the laptop without reading anything. I decided to wait up for her, since
22 she had forgotten her key.

24 At 7:30 p.m. the front doorbell rang. I went to answer and opened the door. It was raining
25 then, but just a drizzle. I saw J.J. standing on the porch. His car, that old black Honda Civic, was
26 parked at the south curb across the street—facing east. He asked for Liza. I stupidly told him
27 she had gone to the Harvard Exit Theater. He wanted to know when she'd be home, and I told
28 him that I wasn't sure. I told him this because I didn't want him bothering her again after what
29 he'd said the night before—he had said that he wouldn't see her again. I was afraid for her. He
30 spoke clearly and calmly. He had something under his right arm. It was in a white plastic bag,
31 but I couldn't tell what it was. He was wearing a sort of black or dark-blue jacket.

33 Later that evening, I sat in the living room reading—although as it got closer to 10:00 p.m.
34 it was hard to concentrate on my book. For one thing, I expected Liza home by 10:00, and
35 I kept looking at my watch because I knew she didn't have her key. I was also a little shaken
36 up by J.J.'s visit earlier that night, so I glanced out the window every now and again to keep
37 an eye out for her. I wasn't able to call her to check in on her because she didn't have her
38 cell phone with her. Around 10:00 p.m. I saw Liza walking up the front walkway. I was so
39 relieved to see her. I went and pulled open the door. Liza had just reached the front porch.
40 She was standing just in front of the porch, about two feet from the step, which is covered by
41 the porch overhang, so she was out of the rain. The front porch lights were on. There is one
42 bracketed light to the left of the door as you are looking out into the street, and there are two
43 overhead recessed lights in the porch ceiling. I also had the lights on in the two front rooms
44 on the first floor, and the blinds were open.

1   Liza had her back to the street. It was raining and dark, cloudy and no moonlight; there was no
2   street light at the curb. But there was a street light at the south curb, across the street—thirty
3   feet west of my front door.

4

5   Just then, I heard a car coming from the west and going east on Prospect. There were no
6   other cars on the street. I looked out and saw a black car—it was a Honda Civic, same style
7   and shape as J.J.'s. You see, I had the door open, and I looked out over Liza's head as she
8   stood down on the porch. The car came on fast, going east. All of a sudden, I heard the brakes
9   squeal, and the car stopped out at the curb right in front of our house.

10

11   I suddenly realized this was J.J.'s car, and then Liza cried out, "Oh no—oh no, Joe!" or something
12   like that. It all happened in a matter of seconds. I saw a man lean out of the front driver's side
13   window—the side facing us. He didn't have a hat on. I saw a small, dark object in his hand,
14   like a gun. Then I heard a shot—only one shot—and I saw Liza fall over backwards. She sort
15   of spun around and fell, with her head towards the street and her feet in the direction of the
16   door. The car sped away down the street, going east. I saw the tail lights, but I couldn't see
17   the license plate number. The motor or engine of this car was running through the whole
18   thing—I could hear it all the time the car was stopped at the curb.

19

20   The first thought that flashed in my mind was that J.J. had shot my daughter. I can positively
21   swear that the face of the man who leaned out of the car was the face of J.J. O'Neill and that
22   it was his car. I saw his face. I saw the car. I know it was J.J. O'Neill. As I told you, I had seen
23   him hundreds of times before, right out there at the curb in that car—the black Honda Civic.
24   And I had seen him there only three hours before. I'm not identifying a stranger I had seen on
25   the night of the murder for the first time; I had seen O'Neill hundreds of times. I knew him; he
26   was no stranger. And I recognized the car, too.

27

28   J.J. O'Neill is definitely the man I saw fire the shot from the car. I saw his face for a couple of
29   seconds, but that was enough. Liza was not blocking my view; she was only 5'6"—I'm 5'11"—
30   and she was standing down on the walkway in front of the porch, while I was at the doorway
31   threshold. The porch is about one foot up from the walkway and the entrance to the house at
32   the doorway threshold is another couple of inches higher. Liza had an umbrella and was just
33   closing it, but she had it down when she turned and faced the street.

34

35   The porch lights were on and there was light from the two front room windows. The car had
36   its headlights on. No, there wasn't any moonlight. It was dark and raining—not hard, but
37   there was some rain on the porch.

38

39   Some neighbors came running over right away and took me into the house. I was in shock.
40   Some police came, but I don't know who called them. One of the police officers—I can't
41   remember his name now—asked me some questions, and I told him pretty much what I've
42   told you. I told him Liza's husband was J.J.—Joseph—O'Neill, and that he lived off of Aurora
43   at 1262 Northgate Way. I said that O'Neill had shot and killed his wife, Liza, my stepdaughter.
44   When the ambulance came to take Liza to the hospital, I rode along, and a doctor there

1   pronounced her dead on arrival. Then I had to identify Liza's body to a woman who said she
2   was the coroner.

4   1.   I'm sure it was 10:00 p.m. when Liza came home from the Harvard Exit Theater,
5   because I had been looking at my watch while waiting for Liza and as I opened the door
6   for her, I heard my clock in the living room strike ten.

8   2.   I only saw O'Neill out there in the car for a few seconds, but I saw the car before that.
9   I saw it coming for about four or five seconds before it stopped. Then I saw O'Neill lean
10 out of the window, take aim, and shoot Liza.

12 3.   September 10 was Liza's birthday. When O'Neill came to the house earlier that night
13 asking for Liza, he didn't say anything to me about her birthday. The package he had under
14 his arm was large enough to a conceal handgun. He didn't have a hat or an umbrella, and
15 his jacket was soaked with rain.

17 4.   One time when J.J. and Liza were dating, he came to the house to see her, and he had
18 a gun with him. I saw it, but I don't know much about guns, so I don't know what kind it
19 was. He said he had been out target shooting with the gun. He claimed he was an expert
20 shot and he liked to practice to make sure his game programs were realistic.

22 5.   I remember that on the morning of September 10, I was checking the voicemail
23 on our home phone. There was a message from O'Neill—I recognized his voice and he
24 sounded angry, but I skipped to the next message. There wasn't anything he had to
25 say that I wanted to hear. I told Liza about the voicemail when she came home. That
26 night at dinner, she said the message was from "Joey." She never said what was in it,
27 and we never discussed it. She must have deleted the message, because I couldn't
28 find it later. I don't know why he wouldn't have just left a message on Liza's cell
29 phone.

31 6.   There's one other thing maybe I should mention, although I'm sure there's no con-
32 nection. My husband, Liza's father, had been a judge for several years before his death.
33 He handled some notorious criminal trials, and I'm sure along the way he made some
34 enemies, particularly some of those he sentenced. I remember one case especially,
35 because I read in the newspaper last August that the person my husband had sentenced
36 had been paroled and was returning to Nita City. That case involved a fairly well-known
37 businessman who was convicted of killing his business associate. There was a lot of
38 publicity and talk of connections with gambling and organized crime. My husband was
39 under a lot of pressure at the trial and sentencing. He said he had to do his duty and
40 do what the law required. The jury found the man—I think his name is John Bierman—
41 guilty, and my husband sentenced him to something like twenty-five to thirty years in
42 prison. This was all about nineteen years ago, just a couple of years before my husband
43 died. At the sentencing, Bierman said he was innocent and that he had been framed by
44 my husband and the prosecutor. He said he'd get revenge for having his life ruined and
45 losing his family in a frame-up if it was the last thing he did. My husband was concerned

1   about this threat at the time, and I remember him talking about it for some time after.
2   I also remember that Bierman had a wife and three children and that she divorced him
3   and left town shortly after he went to prison. Naturally, he also lost his business when
4   he went to prison.

CERTIFICATION BY COURT REPORTER

The above is a true and accurate transcription of (Mrs.) Mary Wilson's testimony at the trial of the case of *State v. O'Neill*, which testimony was recorded stenographically by me at the time it was given.

Signed and Attested to by:

Bill Clarmont

Certified Court Reporter   December 15, YR-1

TESTIMONY OF FRANK NOVAK AT FIRST TRIAL
DECEMBER 16, YR-1

FRANK NOVAK, called to testify on behalf of the State and having been duly sworn, testified as follows:

1 My name is Frank Novak. I am a member of the Nita City Police Department, and I have
2 worked as a police officer for the city for five years.
3
4 On the night of September 10, YR-1, Officer Matt Johnson and I were on duty in Squad
5 Car 15. We were on routine patrol, and at approximately 10:10 p.m. there was a radio call to
6 investigate a shooting at 1704 East Prospect Street. We were in the area and radioed that we
7 would cover the call. We proceeded directly to the Prospect Street address with lights and
8 sirens, arriving at about 10:15 p.m.
9
10 When we got there, I saw some people huddled in the rain in front of 1704 East Prospect
11 Street. We found the victim, a young woman who looked to be in her late twenties or early
12 thirties, lying on the front walkway in front of the house. The front door was open. The victim's
13 feet were pointed toward the door, about six inches from the step up to the porch, and her
14 head was towards the street. She was lying on her back. There was a significant amount of
15 blood from a chest wound. I checked for signs of life. There was a slight pulse in the wrist and
16 jugular vein; the victim was gurgling and gasping. I asked Johnson to administer emergency
17 aid to the victim while I radioed in to confirm that an ambulance had been called and was on
18 its way. They said they would be there momentarily.
19
20 One of the bystanders reported that the victim's mother, Mrs. Mary Wilson, was inside and
21 that she apparently had observed the shooting. Johnson stayed with the victim, and I went
22 inside the house to talk with the mother. When I entered the house, Mrs. Wilson was being
23 comforted by two other women; she was crying and half-hysterical. I calmed her down, and she
24 said that the woman who had been shot was her stepdaughter, Liza. She said that the victim
25 had been shot by a man who came up in a car at the curb in front of the house. She said the
26 man leaned out of the car window and fired a gun at her daughter who was standing on the
27 porch. Mrs. Wilson said she recognized this man as her daughter's estranged husband, Joseph
28 J. O'Neill. She said that O'Neill and her daughter had separated about a month before and that
29 since then her daughter had been living with her at the Prospect Street address. Mrs. Wilson
30 informed me that O'Neill was living at a friend's house located at 1262 Northgate Way.
31
32 As I was talking to Mrs. Wilson the ambulance arrived. I went outside and saw that two
33 additional police cruisers had arrived, and officers had placed first-response evidence markers
34 down around the victim to document her position. The medics lifted the victim onto a gurney
35 and informed me that they were taking her to the Norwegian Medical Center on Capitol Hill.
36 Mrs. Wilson went with the ambulance. I found out later that the victim was pronounced dead
37 on arrival at the hospital. I understand that the coroner, Dr. Elizabeth Martin, is now deceased.

1   After the ambulance left, officers began interviewing the witnesses and processing the
2   scene for evidence. One officer began taking photographs of the scene. The witnesses were
3   neighbors, but none of them had seen anything. They all had heard a single shot.
4
5   In examining the crime scene, I found a bullet on the step in front of the door. I believed it to
6   be a standard 9 mm round. I am familiar with 9 mm bullets—in fact, I own a 9 mm Glock—and
7   the bullet on the porch appeared to be a 9 mm bullet. On examining the door and doorway,
8   I found a mark on the door post where the bullet had apparently struck and then dropped
9   to the step where I picked it up. It had apparently passed through the victim's body and then
10   struck the door post. I put my mark on the bullet and later that evening turned it over to the
11   lab for analysis.
12
13   Johnson had radioed headquarters for instructions. We were advised to contact the victim's
14   husband, Joseph J. O'Neill, to inform him of the shooting and ask him to come to headquarters
15   for further investigation. We left the rest of the police team at the scene to finish processing
16   it and to interview other neighbors on the block to see if anyone had seen anything. We went
17   to the Northgate address that Mrs. Wilson had given me for the victim's husband, Joseph J.
18   O'Neill. We left the Prospect Street house at about 10:30 p.m. and got to 1262 Northgate Way
19   at around 10:45 p.m. The drive took a little over ten minutes; we turned our emergency lights
20   on but did not use our siren at all. The house at 1262 Northgate Way appeared to have several
21   residents. The young woman who answered the door identified herself as Amber Donovan.
22   She said she owned the house and rented two bedrooms and a basement mother-in-law
23   apartment to help pay the mortgage. We identified ourselves as police officers and asked to
24   see Joseph J. O'Neill. She said he rented the mother-in-law apartment and asked us in. When
25   we arrived at the Northgate address I had noticed a black, YR-12 Honda Civic sedan parked
26   at the curb in front of the house, and I asked Ms. Donovan if it was her car. She said no, that
27   it was Joseph J. O'Neill's.
28
29   Amber Donovan told us that Mr. O'Neill's apartment was in the basement, at the bottom of
30   the stairs. We went down and knocked at his door. A man who appeared to be thirty to thirty-
31   five years old opened the door. We were in uniform, and I identified myself by name and said
32   we were Nita City police officers. I asked him his name, and he identified himself as Joseph
33   O'Neill. He asked what this was all about, and I told him that his wife had been shot that
34   night around 10:00 p.m.. I noticed that he turned pale. His face turned a chalky white, and I
35   thought he was going to faint. He asked us to come inside. He was shaken up, and I helped
36   him to sit down in a chair. Right after he sat down in the chair, he said, "Liza's been shot? Is
37   she dead?" I told him that we did not know if she was dead or not and that she had been
38   taken to the hospital by ambulance.
39
40   I then asked O'Neill if he would come to headquarters with us to answer some questions, and
41   he said he would, gladly. He said if we could give him some time to dress, he would go with
42   us to headquarters and help us all he could.
43
44   We followed O'Neill to his bedroom and stood in the doorway while he was getting ready.
45   When we came, O'Neill was dressed in a bathrobe. There was a bed in the room. I noticed

1   that it was made up. It had the comforter and pillows on it and had not been slept in, as far
2   as I could tell.
3
4   While he was dressing, and without any questions from us, O'Neill said that he had been
5   playing a video game on his computer when we came to the door. The screen on his computer
6   monitor was black and his desk chair was pushed in so that the back of the chair was flush
7   with the desk. The room was not tidy when we entered—there was clothing thrown on the
8   floor in a heap: pants, socks, boxer shorts, and a dark-colored jacket—dark blue or black. This
9   jacket was soaking wet. It had been raining heavily off and on that night, and the jacket looked
10 as if it had been just recently worn in the rain.
11
12 Near the jacket I saw a gun. I recognized it as a Glock 17. I looked at it and sort of moved
13 towards it. But then O'Neill, who was putting a shirt on, suddenly jumped in front of me and
14 grabbed the gun. We were alarmed, and I put my hand on my holster, but after he held the
15 gun for a moment or so, he looked at me and handed it to me. He said: "This is mine. I bought
16 it when I was in the service—Army. I use it for target practice." He also told us that he was
17 a video game developer. He said that he had to know all about guns so that he could design
18 popular games, most of which involved guns and other weapons. He told me he had nothing
19 to hide when he handed the gun to me. I examined the gun and pulled back the slide. It had
20 no magazine in it, and there was no round in the chamber. It looked as if it had been cleaned
21 recently. I told O'Neill that I would have to take the gun with me to headquarters. He said,
22 "OK, take it; I've got nothing to hide." Then he picked up the wet jacket and handed it to me.
23 I looked at it and told him that I would have to take the jacket also. And he said, "Sure, go
24 ahead."
25
26 O'Neill then went back to finish dressing. Several times while he was dressing, he said things
27 like, "I have nothing to hide. I want to cooperate with you all the way. I'll be glad to go with
28 you to police headquarters and to help in any way I can." I told him that we appreciated his
29 cooperation. O'Neill acted voluntarily and on his own at all times. We never arrested him or
30 demanded that he come to headquarters with us. He volunteered to do that. And we never
31 asked him any questions. He spoke to us while he was dressing, but it was always at his own
32 initiative.
33
34 As O'Neill was dressing, I noticed that he did not use any of the clothing on the floor. He got
35 dry clothing from a clothes closet. I saw that the pants on the floor were soaking wet with rain
36 and the shoes were muddy and wet. He did not put those shoes on, but got a dry pair from
37 the closet.
38
39 After he had finished dressing he said he was ready to go, and we left his room. We went out
40 the front door of the house. As we were approaching our police car, which was parked behind
41 the black Honda Civic, O'Neill said that he wanted to lock his car. He said that the car was in
42 poor condition and pretty beat up, but it was all he had.
43
44 O'Neill got in the squad car with us, and we proceeded to headquarters. Johnson was driving;
45 I had the jacket and gun with me in the front passenger seat, and O'Neill was in the back.

On the way to headquarters, O'Neill was nervous and agitated. He kept talking to us. He asked, "What really happened to Liza?" I told him that a man had driven up in front of her home at around 10:00 p.m. and fired a shot at her and that she was taken to the hospital by ambulance. O'Neill got very excited and stated that the house on Prospect Street was not her home; that it was her stepmother's, and something about how she shouldn't have been there. He asked how his wife was. I told him that we didn't know and that she had been taken to Norwegian Medical Center. At no time that night, either in the car or in his room, did he ask to be taken to the hospital. On the ride downtown, O'Neill also talked a lot about his being a game developer and how he was always looking to develop good plots for games.

Allen J. Bradley, a homicide detective, was there when we got to headquarters. It was around 11:15 p.m. Bradley took me into a side room. I showed him the gun and the jacket. I told him about our investigation at 1704 East Prospect and what Mrs. Wilson had told me. I also described what had happened in O'Neill's room. Bradley then told me they had word from the hospital that Liza Wilson O'Neill had been pronounced dead on arrival. Bradley and I returned to the room where Joseph J. O'Neill was sitting. Detective Bradley then informed O'Neill that he was under arrest for murder and informed him of his constitutional right to remain silent and to assistance of counsel. Detective Bradley also informed him that he could use the telephone for any purpose. O'Neill signed a waiver form and made a statement.

When O'Neill had finished making his statement, I took him to the crime lab for some tests. Lab technician Weibel was on duty, and he administered a gunshot residue test on O'Neill. Then O'Neill was placed in a cell. I filed the recovered evidence: the gun, jacket, and bullet with the custodian's office and submitted a request to the crime lab for an analysis of the gun and bullet. Homicide detectives also searched O'Neill's apartment and seized many of his possessions, including his car and clothing, and the lab also tested these items.

I understand that the lab analysis of the bullet and gun were inconclusive. The bullet was a 9 mm, as I had observed, but it was too smashed for any comparison ballistics tests. Also, the lab reported that the gun had been cleaned and was wet, and that it was therefore impossible to determine if it had been fired one, two, or even three times after it was cleaned. I imagine it could have been cleaned right after the shooting if the person knew anything about guns.

The gunshot residue tests performed on O'Neill, his car, and his jacket were also inconclusive. I'm not surprised that the gunshot residue tests were inconclusive; they often are. There are many ways to prevent gunpowder particles from showing up when a gunshot residue test is performed. A person can wear gloves or clean his hands or clothing with a chemical agent, like gasoline or any strong "cutting" agent. It is a lot like fingerprints. If a print is left and the comparison is positive, then you know without a doubt the person was there; but if there is no print, it doesn't mean anything, because there are so many ways to prevent prints from being left. when he went to "lock his cer"

The officers at the scene never discovered a spent 9 mm casing, and none was recovered from O'Neill's car, clothing, or apartment. An empty Glock 17 magazine was discovered among the clothes on the floor of his bedroom, and a half-empty box of 9 mm ammunition was found

1   in his closet. I suppose he could have disposed of the spent casing somewhere along the way
2   and put the unused ammunition in the box when he got home.
3
4   I understand that O'Neill was arraigned and pleaded not guilty.
5
6   **ADDITIONAL POINTS**
7
8   1.   Before we left 1704 East Prospect Street on the night of September 10, YR-1, Officer
9   Johnson and I measured the distance from the front door of the house on the porch to the
10 curb on the street. It was thirty-five and a half feet. We used a fifty-foot tape measure.
11
12 2.   When Officer Johnson and I arrived at 1704 East Prospect on the night of September
13 10, we parked our squad car at the curb directly in line with the front door of the house.
14 Our car was pointed east. When I found the 9 mm bullet on the porch, Officer Johnson
15 was sitting in the driver's seat of the squad car calling headquarters for further instruc-
16 tions. I shouted to him that I had found the bullet, and he leaned out of the car window,
17 with his head and shoulders out, looking towards me. I am positive that when I looked
18 at Johnson in the car, I could see him distinctly. I could recognize his face and features at
19 that distance. It wasn't raining then, but it was dark. There was no street light at the curb
20 there, but there was one on the other side of the street, about twenty feet west of where
21 our car was parked.
22
23 3.   No, we didn't give O'Neill any Miranda warnings at his room on Northgate Way.
24 We didn't arrest him, and we didn't ask him any questions. We had been instructed by
25 headquarters to inform him of the shooting and to ask him to come to headquarters for
26 questioning and further investigation. We did just that; we asked him to come, and he
27 volunteered to do so. He spoke to us several times, but we did not ask him any questions.
28
29 4.   No, Mrs. Wilson never said anything to me about a phone message in which O'Neill
30 threatened his wife with violence. I don't know anything about that. Mrs. Wilson left with
31 the ambulance shortly after I arrived. I just talked to her for a few minutes.
32
33 5.   Officer Johnson is deceased. He died of wounds received in a gun battle in a holdup
34 attempt. I was not on duty then and was not with him.

CERTIFICATION BY COURT REPORTER

The above is a true and accurate transcription of Officer Frank Novak's testimony at the trial of the case of *State v. O'Neill*, which testimony was recorded stenographically by me at the time it was given.

Signed and Attested to by:

Bill Clarmont

Certified Court Reporter   December 16, YR-1

TESTIMONY OF JOSEPH J. O'NEILL AT FIRST TRIAL*
DECEMBER 17, YR-1

JOSEPH J. O'NEILL, having taken the stand to testify on his own behalf and having been duly sworn, testified as follows:

1 My name is Joseph J. O'Neill. I am thirty years old. I live at 1262 Northgate Way here in Nita
2 City.
3
4 Yes, I am the defendant in this case, and I know I've been charged with the murder of my wife,
5 Liza O'Neill, on the night of September 10, YR-1. My attorney has advised me that I do not
6 have to testify in my own defense under the Constitution, but I want to waive that right and
7 testify here today. I have nothing to hide. I didn't kill my wife—I loved her.
8
9 **BACKGROUND**
10
11 I am a freelance video game developer. I started my own business a couple of years ago.
12 I don't work for anybody. I am independent and work on my own. My parents died when
13 I was four years old. I was raised by my grandfather and grandmother, my mother's parents,
14 who are now deceased. When I was in high school I got really into gaming. When I graduated
15 from high school I enlisted in the Army because it seemed like a good way to get out of doing
16 the same old boring stuff every day. After my service was done, I returned to Nita City. I had
17 a little money saved, but I didn't know what to do with myself. I started playing games again
18 all the time because going outside sort of freaked me out sometimes. Anyway, I figured that
19 since I was really good at gaming I should learn how to make some money out of it. I got a
20 part-time job at the computer store so I could get software on the cheap, and I lived with my
21 buddy's sister, Amber, to keep my expenses down. I gave all the time I could to my learning
22 how to design games and write code, but I did not sell any of my computer software concepts
23 or game designs until September 10, YR-1.
24
25 I met Liza Wilson in the fall of YR-3. We dated, and in the summer of YR-2 we decided to
26 get married. Liza lived with her stepmother at 1704 East Prospect Street. Her real mother
27 died when she was two years old. Four years later, her father married Mary Wilson, Liza's
28 stepmother. Wicked stepmother, I should say. Liza's father died in YR-12 and Mrs. Wilson took
29 over Liza's life. When I met Liza, she was working as a personal assistant to Gill Bates. I visited
30 the Wilson home many times. From the beginning, Mrs. Wilson hated me. She was rude to me
31 from the start and told me that she was against my marrying Liza. We were married anyway
32 on November 15, YR-2. Liza was interested in my work as a game developer; she thought I had
33 a future in it. It was her idea that I quit my job at the computer store so that I could have more
34 time to follow my dreams. We lived in an apartment at 250 Valley Street. Liza went on with
35 her job at the Bates Fund. She was making about $4,000 a month. She was also getting about
36 $1,000 from a trust fund that her father had set up for her in his will.

---

*Note: Defendant's testimony at the first trial may not be used during the prosecution's case-in-chief. It may be used for impeachment if the defendant elects to take the stand to testify on his own behalf at the second trial.

1 I understand that the main witness against me is Mrs. Wilson. I know she says she saw me fire
2 the shot that killed Liza. But she couldn't have, because I wasn't there. Mrs. Wilson is wrong.
3 For one thing, it was dark and rainy that night. Her hatred of me, her emotional reaction to
4 me, has made her think I was the man who fired the shot. Because of her hatred, she saw
5 what she wanted to see.

MRS. WILSON'S ANIMOSITY TOWARD ME

1. When I was dating Liza Mrs. Wilson repeatedly trashed me. She said more than once
that I wasn't good enough for Liza and that she would do all she could to prevent the marriage. She also repeatedly harped on the fact that she thought I was too old for Liza.

2. We were married by a judge, in spite of Mrs. Wilson's opposition, on November 15,
YR-2. Mrs. Wilson refused to attend either the wedding ceremony or reception. It broke
Liza's heart. Liza begged her to come, but she refused. ← *final evidence of which one*

3. After we were married Liza and I did visit Mrs. Wilson at her home. Shortly after
we were married Liza insisted that I give up my computer store job and spend all my
time working on my computer gaming designs at home. She said she wanted me to
realize my potential and she saw it as an investment in our future together. When we
told Mrs. Wilson about this, right in front of Liza, she accused me of being a "lazy deadbeat" and trying to live off Liza's money. I hated going there.

4. After a while, I stopped going with Liza to Mrs. Wilson's, and Liza would go alone.
She would return home after these visits really depressed and tell me that Mrs. Wilson
was trying to get her to leave me and move back home. After a while, Liza lost interest
in my career. She began to talk to me about getting what she called a "real job" and,
said she could get me some kind of work using her connections to the Bates family.
I saw this as Mrs. Wilson's agenda, not Liza's, and I refused to give up my dream and
our future.

5. Mrs. Wilson finally persuaded Liza to leave me. One night in July YR-1, Liza gave me
an ultimatum. She told me she was going back to Mrs. Wilson's if I did not give up my
gaming. Liza had been the only person who had ever loved and believed in me. I couldn't
believe that she would abandon me and turn her back on our dream. I refused, and we
had a huge fight. She called for a taxi and went to her stepmother's.

6. After that, I'd go to Mrs. Wilson's several times a week to try to persuade Liza to
come back to me. Liza said she would only come back to me if I gave up on my career
and dreams. During these conversations Mrs. Wilson was always present; she insisted on
being there while Liza and I were talking. She repeatedly told Liza not to come back to
me. She actually ordered Liza to divorce me! And again she told me, in front of Liza, that
I was no good and lazy and living off Liza's money. Whenever I tried to get Liza to go out
of the house somewhere so that we could talk things over in private, Mrs. Wilson would
step in.

1   7. It is true that during these conversations I sometimes lost my temper. I accused
2   Mrs. Wilson of breaking up my marriage. She had poisoned Liza's mind against me
3   and was committed to keeping us apart. She hated me, not because of anything I did,
4   but because I wasn't some smart, rich, fraternity boy like she thought Liza should
5   be with.
6
7   **EVENTS OF SEPTEMBER 9, YR-1**
8
9   The last time I saw Liza alive was on the night of September 9, YR-1. I went to Mrs. Wilson's
10   between 9:00 and 10:00 p.m., and I only stayed a little while. Mrs. Wilson and Liza were there.
11   I don't remember the exact words anyone said, but the gist of it was that I asked Liza "for
12   the last time" to come back to me. She still refused; unless I gave up my work. I would not
13   do that, and I said, "So that's it? We're all through then. I'm sorry it didn't work out." I admit
14   I was angry at Mrs. Wilson and Liza. I do remember I said something about making them both
15   sorry for what they had done to me, and that Mrs. Wilson had ruined my marriage and that
16   I'd make her pay for it. I don't recall the exact words, but what I meant was that when I sold
17   my first blockbuster video game, they would regret what they had done. I didn't mean I'd do
18   physical violence to them. I left the house at about 9:30 p.m.
19
20   As I recall, during this conversation Mrs. Wilson kept saying something about how Liza would
21   be a "fool" to come back to me.
22
23   After I left them I drove around the streets for a while trying to think things out. I was confused,
24   hurt, and upset. I loved my wife, and I wanted us to be together. Her stepmother was the
25   cause of our problems. The more I thought of it, the angrier I got at the old witch.
26
27   When I got back to Amber's house, where I had gone to live after Liza left me, I was really
28   upset. I tried to reach Liza on her cell phone but my call went directly to voicemail. I then
29   called her home number but it went to voicemail too. I left a message because I wanted her
30   stepmother to know exactly how I felt. I don't recall exactly what I said, but I do remember
31   saying something about making them regret what they had done to me. Then I sent an e-mail
32   to Liza telling her the same thing. I suppose they will bring these messages up as evidence
33   against me, but I didn't mean physical violence. I only meant that Mrs. Wilson would regret
34   what she had done when I became a successful programmer and that Liza would regret
35   listening to her.
36
37   **EVENTS OF SEPTEMBER 10, YR-1**   *check*
38
39   September 10, YR-1, was Liza's birthday. That afternoon I got a letter from a big Bay Area
40   video game company, Tsunami Entertainment. It had a check in it for $2,500 as an advance
41   for a video game concept that I had pitched them—they wanted to produce it. I was so
42   happy—I had finally gotten the big break I needed to get into the industry. I felt like the weight
43   of the world had been lifted from my shoulders and the sun was shining on me for the first
44   time in a long time. I was sure that with this good news I could win Liza back. I cashed the
45   check and went to Nordstrom to buy Liza a shoulder bag that I knew she had wanted for the

1   past couple of months. The bag was a present for Liza's birthday. I went back to the house on
2   Northgate and paid Amber the part of the rent I still owed her for the past month.
3
4   That night I drove to Mrs. Wilson's Prospect Street house—I drive a black, YR-12 Honda Civic.
5   I wanted to surprise Liza. I got to their house at about 7:30 p.m., but I'm not positive about
6   the time.
7
8   I parked at the south curb across the street from 1704 East Prospect, My car pointed east.
9   There is a single porch light on a bracket on one side of the door, about five feet up from
10   the ground and two recessed lights right above the front porch. Both sets of lights were on.
11   Mrs. Wilson came to the door, and I asked for Liza. She told me that Liza had gone to the
12   Harvard Exit Theater, an art-house movie theater where Liza and I had often gone. I asked
13   when she would be back, and Mrs. Wilson said around 10:00 p.m. I did not tell Mrs. Wilson
14   about having sold my game concept. I only talked to her for a few minutes at the most; she
15   was rude and short with me—I was still hoping to surprise Liza with the news, and I didn't
16   think it would change Mrs. Wilson's opinion of me anyway. She did not ask me in, of course; it
17   was raining, and she made me just stand there in the rain. I didn't have a hat or an umbrella,
18   and I was getting pretty wet. I had the Nordstrom box under my arm. I didn't want it to get
19   wet so I had wrapped it in a plastic grocery bag. *what did he do with bag*
20
21   I left Mrs. Wilson's at about 7:35 p.m. or so and drove to find Liza at the movie theater.
22   I thought I would try to surprise Liza there. While I was driving I was trying to think things out.
23   The idea that I would lose Liza because of Mrs. Wilson upset me. I couldn't see myself living
24   without her. I was in love with my wife. It seemed so cruel and ironic really that I should lose
25   her by one day after holding out so long. I did not want to go on without Liza so I decided
26   to make one more attempt to talk to her. I hoped that with my success, and without her
27   stepmother's interference, we could get back together.
28
29   I parked about a block from the theater. I knew the woman at the ticket window, Maria
30   Vargas. I had met her a couple of times when Liza and I went there because she was a friend
31   of Liza's from Nita State. I think it was about 7:45 p.m. or so when I arrived. The ticket window
32   is right on the street in front of the theater. I went up to the window and asked Maria if she
33   had seen Liza. I told her I had been to Mrs. Wilson's and that Mrs. Wilson had told me that
34   Liza had gone to the Harvard Exit Theater. Maria said that Liza was inside. I remember asking
35   Maria several times when the show would be over. I think she said the first show would be
36   over at about 9:40 or 9:45 p.m. We talked for a while. Maria said something about Liza being
37   "afraid" of me, or something like that. I told Maria that there was nothing wrong between
38   Liza and me, but that it was all Mrs. Wilson's fault. I said that Mrs. Wilson was an evil person
39   who had broken up my marriage and that my marriage would be OK if Mrs. Wilson were not
40   in the way.
41
42   I bought a ticket and went into the lobby. I was going to wait for Liza. I waited a while and
43   then went to the men's room. I was thinking about selling my game concept that day and
44   how, if it hadn't been for Mrs. Wilson, everything would be perfect and Liza and I would be
45   sharing the success. I decided to go into the theater and look for her. There were quite a few

1   people in there and with the lights down and the small screen, I could hardly see anything.
2   From behind and in the dark it was hard to tell people apart. I saw a woman I thought might
3   be Liza sitting next to a tall man. I got pretty upset and started to feel foolish. I didn't want
4   to make a scene and disturb the movie so I went outside and took some deep breaths. Once
5   I calmed down, I decided that I might as well leave and try to patch things up with Liza the
6   following day. I got in my car and drove east for about ten minutes. I think it was about 8:30
7   p.m.—I am sorry I can't be precise about the time—and I went into the Deluxe Bar and Grille.
8
9   I had three beers at the bar. There were about thirty-five people in there. I was there for
10   about forty-five minutes as best as I can remember. I talked with the bartender—I don't know
11   his name. He was busy serving all the other customers, so we didn't talk continuously. I did
12   not tell him my name, but I do recall telling him I was a video game developer. And I did say
13   something about my mother-in-law having broken up my marriage and poisoning my wife's
14   mind against me so much that she had left me. I recall I said that my mother-in-law hated me,
15   and maybe I said I hated her too for all she had done to me. I was pretty pissed off at the time.
16   I couldn't get the thought out of my head that, now that I'd finally made it with my career, Liza
17   and I were separated.
18
19   After about an hour, I think, I left the bar. I was certainly not drunk. I went to my car and
20   sat in it a while before driving off. I can't say exactly how long it was, but I think that I left
21   there at about 9:30 p.m. I was trying to decide whether to go back to Liza's or to go home.
22   Finally, I decided to go see my friend Sam Russo, who lives on that side of town near Mrs.
23   Wilson's and pick up my gun. Sam is a friend of mine from the video gaming club we both
24   belong to, "The Guild." I first met him through his brother Jim, who has been my gunsmith
25   for many years—I always take my gun to Jim for cleaning and repairs. Jim knew about my
26   interest in video games and introduced me to his brother, who is also a hard-core gamer. I
27   would often give Sam my gun when it needed to be cleaned, since he lives with his brother,
28   to save myself a trip.
29
30   I bought this gun when I was in the service, and kept it as a memento of my service days.
31   The only time I used it was to practice target shooting at a gun range on the outskirts of
32   Nita City. Since I develop video games, and many of them involve guns, I thought I ought to
33   be familiar with guns as part of my business. I used to practice a couple of times a week,
34   shooting at paper targets. Besides gaming, it's my only hobby. I became an expert shot; I
35   used to tell people I could hit a dime at 100 yards, although, that's not really possible with
36   a handgun. I was just bragging, I guess. Liza knew I had the gun. I used to keep the gun in
37   my bedside table, but after Liza and I moved in together she asked me to put it in a more
38   secure location. After that, I started using one of her sweater boxes to store my gun and
39   ammunition. When I moved back to the Northgate house I put that box on the top shelf of
40   my bedroom closet.
41
42   I drove down Roy Street on the way to Sam's house. I passed the theater but didn't stop;
43   I didn't even look over to the ticket booth as I passed. I turned right on Prospect and drove by
44   the Wilson house; the porch lights and the lights in the two front rooms were on. It was still
45   drizzling rain.

1   I got to Sam Russo's house at 2388 East Prospect. I had left the gun with him for cleaning and
2   some minor repairs—the trigger return spring had busted—about a week before. The lights
3   were still on, so I knocked on the door. Sam let me in and we talked for a few minutes. I could
4   tell he was getting ready for bed, though, so I didn't stay long. Sam got the gun for me—when
5   he gave me the gun, I did not notice that there were two bullets left in the magazine. I guess
6   I had left them in the gun when I gave it to him. Sam reminded me about the bullets in the
7   magazine when he gave me the gun and told me to be careful. I took the magazine out of the
8   gun and put it in my pants pocket. I put the gun in my jacket pocket, paid the bill—$47.50—
9   and left. I was only there for a few minutes. You can check that out with Sam. I got in my car
10 and drove back to my place on Northgate. I was never near the Wilson house again that night.
11
12 I went down to my apartment in the basement of Amber's house. I took off my wet clothes
13 and got into a bathrobe and pajamas. I put the two bullets back in my ammunition box in the
14 closet—I never leave the gun loaded because Amber has a kid. I sat down at my computer
15 to mess around with a game. I had developed a headache that wouldn't go away and
16 around 10:15 or 10:30 I went upstairs to see if Amber had some aspirin. She was watching TV
17 in the living room on the first floor. That room faces the street. She gave me some Advil, and
18 I went back down to my room.
19
20 Around 10:45, I think it was, I heard a knock on my door. I opened the door, and there were
21 two men there in police uniforms. One asked me my name. I told him my name and I said,
22 "What's this all about?" He said that my wife had been shot. That really shook me up. I asked,
23 "Is she dead?" He said that they did not know whether she was dead or not but that she had
24 been taken to the hospital by ambulance.
25
26 The cops asked me if I would go to police headquarters with them, and I said I would gladly do
27 so. I told them if they would let me dress, I would go with them and help all I could.
28
29 I went to get some dry clothing from my closet. When I came in earlier that night I had thrown
30 my wet clothing on the floor. As I went to get some clothes from the closet, I noticed my wet
31 jacket on the floor and, right alongside it, my gun. I guess it had fallen out of my pocket when
32 I dropped my jacket on the floor.
33
34 I saw one of the cops sort of move over to pick up the gun, but I picked it up before he got it.
35 I was afraid I was going to get into trouble because I didn't have the gun registered, so I picked
36 it up. But then I handed it over to him. I said, "I have nothing to hide, officer." I handed him
37 the jacket too. I told him again, "I have nothing to hide. You take them."
38
39 The cops did not force me to go with them; they did not arrest me. They asked me to go
40 downtown to headquarters, and I went with them voluntarily. I felt at all times that I was free
41 to go with them or refuse to go with them. Neither of these officers at any time said anything
42 to me about having a lawyer, remaining silent, or that anything I said might be used against
43 me, etc.

[handwritten margin note, left]: if he had to grab the gun where are the fingerprints

[handwritten note above line 34]: His word against officers

1　I told them I had bought the gun while in the service and that I used it for target shooting.
2　I told them I designed video games and that I had to know a lot about guns for my work.
3
4　I finished dressing and went to the station in the police car. They did not force me to do this.
5　A man at the station, who said he was a homicide detective, told me my wife was dead—dead
6　on arrival at the hospital. The detective went into a room with one of the cops. When he came
7　out he told me that I was being arrested for the murder of my wife. He said that I had the
8　right to remain silent, that anything I said might be used against me, and that I had the right
9　to call a lawyer. I signed a form and made a statement. I told them I had absolutely nothing to
10　do with my wife's murder, and I knew nothing about the shooting. I told them what I did that
11　night and how I certainly wasn't near the Wilson house on Prospect Street at the time of the
12　shooting. I told them I was at Sam Russo's shop and then I went right home. I told them to
13　check this with Sam Russo and Amber Donovan. I went right home from Russo's shop; I wasn't
14　near the Wilson house at 10:00 p.m., and I certainly didn't shoot my wife.
15
16　After I made the statement, one of the cops took me to the crime lab, and one of the
17　technicians performed a test on my hands. At the lab, the technician put some sticky crap on
18　my hands and performed a test. I think it's called a gunshot residue test.
19
20　I was arraigned in court and have been staying in jail, because the bond is too high for me to
21　get out. I was permitted to visit the funeral parlor under police escort to see my wife's body.
22
23　I didn't kill my wife. I loved her.
24
25　**ADDITIONAL POINTS**
26
27　1.　Amber has been a good friend to me. She was interested in my career, and she has
28　often let me pay the rent late when I was a little short of funds. I have paid her all I
29　owed her.
30
31　2.　My apartment in Amber's house has a separate entrance out to the alley in the back,
32　but I never use it. I keep it locked from the inside, and I always use the front door at the
33　top of the stairs.
34
35　3.　As a member of the club of gamers that we both belong to, called "The Guild," Sam
36　Russo certainly knows my reputation.
37
38　4.　Yes, although I have never seen it, Liza did explain to me several times the terms of her
39　father's will. Under it, Liza was the beneficiary of a trust fund that had been set up for her.
40　Judge Wilson's property went to Mrs. Wilson just during her life time, and, after that, to
41　Liza. As I understand it, if Liza was dead when Mrs. Wilson died, then all the property goes
42　to the one named in Liza's will. Soon after we were married Liza insisted that she make a
43　will. That will left everything to me.

CERTIFICATION BY COURT REPORTER

The above is a true and accurate transcription of the defendant Joseph J. O'Neill's testimony at the trial of the case of *State v. O'Neill*, which testimony was recorded stenographically by me at the time it was given.

Signed and Attested to by:

Bill Clarmont

Certified Court Reporter   December 17, YR-1

STATEMENT OF MARIA VARGAS
(WITNESS FOR THE STATE)

1   My name is Maria Vargas. I live at 50 King Street, Nita City. I am not married. I am employed
2   at Nita Elementary School as a teacher. I also volunteer as a lobby manager at the Harvard
3   Exit Theater—an art-house theater that shows mostly independent and foreign films. I'm a
4   board member of the nonprofit that runs the theater, the Nita Film Society. The Harvard Exit
5   is in the historic Poseidon Theater building on the south side of Roy Street—it's about fifteen
6   blocks west of Mrs. Mary Wilson's residence at 1704 East Prospect Street. I was working the
7   ticket window there on September 10, YR-1. I understand Joseph J. O'Neill is charged with the
8   murder of his wife, Liza, on that day. I was not a witness to this terrible thing, but I knew Liza
9   and J.J., and I saw both of them that night.
10
11 Liza and I were pretty close friends. I went to college with her at Nita State. We moved back to Nita
12 City when we graduated and I often visited her home at 1704 East Prospect Street. I also knew
13 her stepmother, Mrs. Wilson. Liza's mother died when Liza was two. Two years later her father
14 married his second wife, Mary Wilson. Liza's stepmother raised her. There were no other children.
15
16 I first met J.J. O'Neill in the winter of YR-2 when he and Liza came to the theater, and she
17 introduced him to me. They came to the theater often after that. That summer, Liza told me
18 they were going to get married. The wedding was in November, YR-2. I went to it—it was
19 small and quiet, but pleasant. We all noticed that Mrs. Wilson did not attend.
20
21 Just before they were married Liza told me that Mrs. Wilson was totally against her marrying
22 J.J., but she said they were going to do it anyway. I have the highest respect for Mrs. Wilson's
23 character and reputation. Mrs. Wilson always treated Liza as her own daughter, and Liza's
24 welfare came first with her. She raised Liza as her own, and Liza always referred to her as
25 "mom." I'm sure if Mrs. Wilson objected to Liza's marrying J.J., she did this out of a sense of
26 conscience and duty, to warn Liza and to advise her for her own good. But I admit that from
27 what I heard, the marriage did create a strain in the relationship between Liza and her mother
28 and between Mrs. Wilson and J.J. O'Neill.
29
30 After they were married I didn't see Liza and J.J. at the theater very often. But in August, YR-1,
31 Liza came one night and told me she and J.J. had separated and that she was back living with
32 Mrs. Wilson. She said J.J. was renting a room from the sister of one of his friends. She also
33 told me that J.J. was seeing her at Mrs. Wilson's and trying to get her to come back to him.
34 She said he would get angry and make threats against Mrs. Wilson. He hated her for, as he
35 said, "breaking up his marriage." Liza said he had even turned against her for leaving him. He
36 accused Mrs. Wilson of "poisoning Liza's mind against him" and blamed Liza for listening to
37 Mrs. Wilson.
38
39 I remember that night in August quite well, because I hadn't seen Liza very much since she
40 and J.J. got married. Also, I was surprised to hear that they had separated. Liza and I had been
41 friends for more than a decade, and I was concerned for her happiness.

1   I next saw her on the night of September 10, YR-1. She came up to the ticket window to buy
2   a ticket at about 7:00 p.m. We talked for a few minutes. I noticed that she was frightened
3   and nervous; she kept looking up and down the street as if she expected someone. I asked
4   if she had seen J.J., and she said he had come to the house the night before and threatened
5   Mrs. Wilson again. She said this time he had also threatened her and she was afraid something
6   terrible was going to happen to her and her mother. She said, "J.J. has been making awful
7   threats against us. He has a violent temper, and he might try to do something violent to us."
8   She said that she had told J.J. they were through and that J.J. hated them both now.
9
10 I don't remember her exact words—only the substance of what she said. I recall that she
11 said J.J was furious with her. He accused her of having her mind poisoned against him by that
12 "evil witch," her mother. She said she had received a letter from him that day and that he
13 made terrible threats against her and her mother in the letter. She seemed to be frightened
14 of J.J. Just then, some other people came up to the window, and Liza got her ticket and went
15 into the theater.
16
17 At about 7:45 p.m. J.J. came to the ticket window. I can't be sure about the exact time. He
18 asked me if I had seen Liza. He said he had been to Mrs. Wilson's, and she told him that
19 Liza had gone to the Harvard Exit Theater. I told him she had gone into the show at about
20 7:00 p.m. I said, "J.J., what have you done to Liza? Why don't you leave her alone? She's afraid
21 of you." He told me, "There is nothing wrong between Liza and me. It's her stepmother who's
22 responsible for ruining our marriage. She's not going to get away with it." And he said, "If it
23 weren't for her, we'd be together now. She always hated me. Believe me, they will be sorry
24 for all this, but I hope it isn't too late. I love my wife, and it would be all right between us if
25 her mother weren't in our way." Again, I can only give you the substance of what he said, not
26 the exact words. He asked me when the show would be over, and I told him about 9:40 p.m.
27 I recall that J.J. repeated the question, "Are you sure it will be over at 9:40?"
28
29 J.J. seemed angry, especially when he spoke of Mrs. Wilson. He also seemed nervous. He
30 didn't have a hat on and wasn't carrying an umbrella, although it had been raining off and
31 on during the evening. He wore a black or dark-colored jacket, which was wet, and he had a
32 package under his arm. From what I could see, it looked like a box—not a moving box, but the
33 kind of box you get from stores for Christmas gifts and stuff— in a plastic bag.
34
35 J.J. bought a ticket and went into the theater, but I saw him leave about 8:30 or 8:45 p.m.
36
37 Liza came out when the show ended at about 9:40, and I talked to her for a few minutes. She
38 asked me if J.J. had been there. I told her he had; that he had bought a ticket and gone into
39 the show and then left about 8:30 or 8:45. She asked me whether he had asked for her, and
40 I said he had, and I told her all that he had said to me. She looked really scared. I remember
41 she asked me if I was sure he had left. Then she asked, "Did he have a gun with him?" I was
42 shocked at a question like that; I didn't know what she was talking about. I told her, "Of course,
43 he didn't have a gun." I said if she was frightened we could call the police and that they would
44 see to it that she got home safely. And I said if she didn't want to do this, she could stay with
45 me in the booth until the second show was over, and I'd walk home with her or we could take

1 a cab. But she said she would go home, and she wouldn't call a cab or let me call one. She said
2 good night and walked east on the south side of Roy Street. I never saw her alive again.
3
4 **ADDITIONAL POINTS**
5
6   1.   Yes, I think the box J.J. had under his arm was big enough to have held a gun.
7
8   2.   When J.J. was at the theater the night Liza was killed he didn't say anything to me
9 about the project he was working on. From what I understand, J.J. works on some sort
10 of video games—programming and story development—something to do with guns and
11 gang violence, I think.
12
13   3.   Liza left the theater at about 9:45 p.m. It's about fifteen blocks to her house.
14
15   4.   I remember that when J.J. and Liza were at the theater in the spring of YR-2, they
16 stood at the ticket booth talking with me for a few minutes. There was a western film
17 showing that night, and J.J. was joking about the film. He told me, "I can shoot as well as
18 anyone. I can hit a dime at 100 yards." And Liza said, "I keep telling him he should give up
19 his target-shooting. He's always out with that gun."
20
21   5.   One time before Liza and J.J. ever met—I think it was in the spring of YR-3—I drove
22 to the Wilson house to see Liza. I parked the car at the curb in front of the house, and
23 before I got out of the car I looked up at the front porch. I could easily see Mrs. Wilson
24 from where I was; she was standing on the porch there in front of her front door, and
25 I was leaning out of the window of the car. The front door is about thirty-five feet
26 from the curb. Mrs. Wilson called out, "Hello, Maria. Liza is waiting for you." This was
27 before I got out of the car. It was about 9:30 p.m., and it wasn't raining. On one side
28 of the front door was a bracket light, about five feet up from the floor. It made it easy
29 for me to see Mrs. Wilson. Of course, we had seen each other many times before this.
30 As I recall, it was a bright, moonlit night, and there were no street lights at the curb
31 where I was parked. There was a street light at the opposite curb, on the other side of
32 the street, but that was about twenty-five feet west of where I was parked. I only men-
33 tion this because I understand there is some question about Mrs. Wilson seeing J.J. fire
34 the shot at Liza. I understand that J.J. supposedly drove up in his car, parked in front
35 of the house, and leaned out of the car and shot Liza, who was up on the porch with
36 Mrs. Wilson.

I have read the above statement and it is true and correct.

Name: *Maria Vargas*

Date: September 28, YR-1

Witness: *Paul Jones*

Date: September 28, YR-1

STATEMENT OF AMBER DONOVAN
(WITNESS FOR THE DEFENDANT)

1   My name is Amber Donovan. I live at 1262 Northgate Way, Nita City. I own my home and rent
2   two of the bedrooms and the basement mother-in-law apartment to help pay my mortgage.
3   I am thirty-six years old and divorced. I have a son, Travis, who is nine years old. My ex and
4   I bought the house on Northgate when we got married, but he left when our son was two.
5   It's really just as well that he left because he drank a lot and could never keep a job. I haven't
6   heard from him in years. I work as a clerk at the Nita City Department of Licensing.
7
8   I understand that Joseph J. O'Neill is charged with shooting and killing his wife, Liza, on
9   September 10, YR-1.
10
11   I first met J.J. O'Neill in the fall of YR-4, when he started renting the mother-in-law apartment
12   in my house. J.J. worked with my brother, Chris, at a computer store in town. He grew up in
13   Nita City, graduated from Nita City High School, and had just finished serving in the Army. He
14   didn't leave the house much, except to go to his job. When he was at home, he spent most
15   of his time playing video games. He told me he was doing research because he wanted to
16   become a game designer.
17
18   When he lived at my house before he and Liza got married, he worked most days and spent
19   the nights with his games. He would tell my son and my brother about his ideas for new
20   games and from what I understand, they both thought he had really cool ideas. J.J. was a
21   great renter, and he never caused any trouble. He was quiet and pretty clean for a guy his age.
22   If he drank, I never saw it, and I never heard him come home drunk or anything. I wish I could
23   always find renters as reliable as J.J.
24
25   When J.J. was at my place before his marriage, he was in pretty rough shape financially.
26   A couple of times I gave him credit or a loan for the rent. He would always tell me in advance
27   if he couldn't pay the rent on time, and tell me when he would be able to pay. He was a nice,
28   reliable person, and I thought he could really make something of himself with the ambition
29   he had as a video game designer. He always paid me what he owed exactly when he said he
30   would, and he was great with Travis. In fact, he was happy to watch Travis for me whenever
31   I had to run errands or something.
32
33   He left my place in November, YR-2, when he married Liza Wilson. He owed me $850, which
34   he paid back a couple of weeks after he was married. I guess he got it from his wife. She
35   worked for Gill Bates, which I guess is a pretty cushy job. He told me that he had quit his job
36   at the computer store and was going to be able to devote all of his time to his business. He
37   and Liza lived in an apartment on Valley Street. I recall that before he was married, he told me
38   that Mrs. Wilson, the girl's stepmother, was opposed to the marriage and had tried to prevent
39   it. He said Mrs. Wilson hated him. J.J. and Liza were married before a judge. I attended the
40   wedding, and it was nice. I didn't meet Liza's mother, Mrs. Wilson. I guess she didn't go to the
41   wedding.

1   I did not see J.J. for a long time after that—not until July YR-1, in fact. At that time, he asked to
2   have the apartment again. Since it had just become vacant, I welcomed him back. He said he
3   and Liza had separated and that she was living with her stepmother at her childhood home on
4   Prospect Street. J.J. blamed Liza's mother for breaking up his marriage. He said that she had
5   worked on Liza and influenced her to leave him and that he would never forgive that woman
6   for what she'd done to their marriage.

7

8   He also mentioned that maybe a separation was best until he got on his feet financially.
9   J.J. was very mature. He also said that he had not given up hope that Liza would come back.
10   He thought she would, if Mrs. Wilson would leave them alone and stop interfering with their
11   relationship. I remember him saying that she couldn't live forever and so there was hope that
12   it would turn out all right for Liza and him. Sometime after they separated, J.J. told me that
13   Liza would inherit all her father's property when Mrs. Wilson died, because under the will
14   Mrs. Wilson only had it for her life. He said something about how Mrs. Wilson had robbed Liza
15   of her inheritance and her happiness. He had been thinking about Liza and was kind of down
16   and depressed when he mentioned that.

17

18   When he first came back to my place he said that he was going to devote all his time to his
19   work so he could show Mrs. Wilson and Liza that he could be successful. He said that he had
20   a little money saved, but I don't know where he got it. I didn't ask him about it.

21

22   J.J. had an old, beat-up, black, YR-12 Honda Civic. He used to park it at the curb in front of
23   my place. He lived at my place from July to September, YR-1, and during this time I know he
24   frequently went to the Wilson house to try to get Liza to come back to him. I often saw him
25   leave for there in his car. He told me that he went there about two or three times a week
26   but that Mrs. Wilson was doing her best to prevent any reconciliation between Liza and him.
27   He would come back from these visits very down and depressed, but he wouldn't talk much
28   about what had happened, even though we were good friends and talked a lot.

29

30   Early in the evening of September 9, YR-1—I can't recall the precise time, but it was after
31   6:00 p.m.—J.J. said he was going to see Liza again and make one final effort to get her back.
32   He said, "This is it. This is the last chance I'll give her." I saw him leave. He came back about
33   10:30 p.m..; I heard him come in. My bedroom is on the main floor, and I was in bed. I heard
34   him go down the stairs to his room. The stairs go right down to the basement, and his room
35   is at the bottom of the stairs.

36

37   I distinctly recall September 10, YR-1. That morning J.J. came up and talked to me at about
38   8:30. He said that the night before Liza had refused finally and positively to return to him
39   unless he gave up his game designing idea and got another job. He said he would not do this
40   and that he and Liza were through. He said that he would make them sorry for what they
41   both had done to him, especially that evil old woman who had succeeded in breaking up his
42   marriage. Without her interference he said they could have worked things out. Then he said
43   something about hoping the old lady died soon, because maybe then Liza would come back
44   and they could be happy again.

1   Later that morning, he showed me a check for $2,500 he had received in the mail and said it
2   was an advance for one of his game concepts. He was absolutely thrilled. He said, "I'm on my
3   way at last. They are going to be sorry for what they did to me and for the way they treated
4   me. I've finally made it." He went out to cash the check, and then he came back and paid me
5    $400 he owed me for part of last month's rent. He said he was going to go over that night
6   to see Liza and tell her about his good news. He mentioned that September 10 was Liza's
7   birthday.
8
9   As I said, his apartment is in the basement at the bottom of the stairs from the entrance hall.
10   The living room is on the main floor at the top of the stairs, and my bedroom is right behind
11   it. The door of my living room is right at the top of the stairs, and anybody going out to the
12   street has to go by the living room door to go out the front door.
13
14   On the evening of September 10, YR-1, I met J.J. at the front door when I was coming in from
15   shopping. It was about 7:15 p.m. He had a package wrapped in a white plastic grocery bag.
16   I asked if I could see it, but he said no. I figured it was a birthday present for Liza because it
17   looked to be about the size of a department store box.
18
19   He seemed quiet and down when I saw him leave at about 7:15 p.m. I was surprised at this
20   because he had been so cheerful when the letter with the check came earlier in the day.
21   And he was usually a cheerful, joking, and talkative person. He sure didn't look like a happy
22   husband on the way to celebrate his wife's birthday, but then, I guess with the separation and
23   the problems with Mrs. Wilson he had reason to be down, even though it had been a big day
24   for him professionally. I felt sorry for him, and I hoped that things would turn out all right for
25   him and Liza.
26
27   I looked out and saw him get in his car at the curb. As he drove off he waved to me. He left at
28   about 7:15 p.m. or a little later. I am not positive now, and I can't fix the time more precisely.
29
30   That night I was watching TV in my living room. The door leading to the hall was open. While
31   I was watching TV, I heard a car pull up at the curb outside my front window and the heard the
32   brakes sort of grind or screech. I thought, "Wow, J.J. is certainly in a hurry tonight." I looked
33   out my front window, and I saw his car at the curb and J.J. running up the walk. It was still
34   raining. I heard him unlock the front door and saw him go past my living room entrance. He
35   was in a hurry; he ran up the steps and didn't look into the living room. I didn't notice whether
36   he was carrying anything or not. He may have had something under his arm, for all I could see.
37
38   I'd say that he came in somewhere between 9:40 and 9:55 p.m. I recall the time because
39   I remember I was watching a TV program, which comes on at nine and ends at ten. After
40   the first half hour, there is always a series of commercials and a station break, and that had
41   already been on when I heard J.J.'s car and saw him go past. They always have a preview of
42   the next week's show at 9:55 p.m., and that hadn't come on yet when J.J. got home. I clearly
43   remember that the show hadn't ended yet. I was watching the TV and not my watch or the
44   time, and so I can't say exactly what time J.J. got home that night, but I can fix the time as

1 being somewhere between 9:40 and 9:55. It had to be at least 9:40, because it was pretty
2 close to the end of the show when J.J. got home.
3
4 I did not see him again until around 10:30 p.m. when he came into the living room. I was still
5 watching TV. He was dressed in sweats and slippers. He told me he had a bad cold coming
6 on from being out in the rain so much that night. He said he had been outside and got his
7 clothing soaked. He was feeling down, and he was coughing. I gave him some Advil. He did
8 not say much of anything else and he went back downstairs.
9
10 At about 10:45 p.m., police officers came to the door and introduced themselves as Officers
11 Johnson and Novak. They said they were from the Nita City Police Department and wanted
12 to talk to Joseph O'Neill. I told them his apartment was at the bottom of the stairs in the
13 basement, and they went down. I did not go with them.
14
15 A little while later I saw the police officers and J.J. leave. I stayed in my living room. I didn't say
16 anything to them, and none of them said anything to me.
17
18 I did not hear J.J.'s car being used again that night after I had heard him come in while I was
19 watching TV, around 9:45. After the police left with him I looked out and saw J.J.'s car at the
20 curb. It was parked right where I had seen it before when I looked out. After J.J. had come in
21 earlier I closed the blinds in my front window, and I did not look out the window again until
22 after the police and J.J. left. I can't swear absolutely that J.J.'s car had not been moved or used
23 in the meantime; it's possible that J.J.'s car was moved or used, and I would not have heard
24 it. There is a separate entrance from the mother-in-law apartment, and it leads to an alley in
25 the back of my place. Of course, it would be impossible for me sitting in my living room on the
26 first floor to hear any person using the back door.
27
28 Yes, it rained pretty hard that night from 7:00 to around 10:30 p.m., I think. But whether the
29 rain had stopped any time in between and then started up again, I simply do not know.
30
31 In all the time I knew him, J.J. impressed me as an honest, truthful, and industrious person.
32 I never heard a single bad thing against his character or reputation. I didn't know many of his
33 friends or acquaintances, other than my brother. It seems totally unlikely to me, knowing him
34 as I did and having observed his conduct so often, that he could be guilty of the terrible crime
35 they've charged him with. He's not the kind of person who would do that.
36 *says she knows him but doesn't even know about the gun?*
37 I don't know anything about J.J. owning a gun of any sort. I never saw one in his room or in his
38 possession. Also, I don't know anything about his being an expert shot or shooting for target
39 practice.
40
41 I suppose that if I testify in this case, they will try to mention that I pleaded guilty to a charge
42 of receiving stolen property in June, YR-5. That happened when a man named Jack Swanson
43 rented a room from me for a short time in the spring of YR-5. In May, YR-5, he showed me a
44 diamond ring and offered to sell it to me for $600. At this time, he owed me $450 in rent, and
45 he didn't have any money, so he offered me the ring to pay his bill. He moved right after I took

1   the ring to settle his debt. A few weeks later, the police came to see me and told me the ring
2   had been stolen by Swanson. I had sold it to a jeweler shortly after I got it, and I was charged
3   with "receiving stolen property." I hired a lawyer, Mr. Paul Miller, to defend me. He is dead
4   now. I told him that I didn't know the ring had been stolen when Jack gave it to me. Mr. Miller
5   arranged a deal with the prosecutor where I pled guilty and was given a suspended sentence
6   of one year. There is absolutely nothing else on my record.

I have read the above statement and it is true and correct.

goto later

Name: *Amber Donovan*

Date: October 16, YR-1

Witness: <u>Jack Peters</u>

Date: October 16, YR-1

STATEMENT OF SAM RUSSO
(WITNESS FOR DEFENDANT)

1   My name is Sam Russo. I live with my brother, Jim Russo, at 2388 East Prospect Street, Nita

2   City, Nita. I am forty-six years old, and I am not married. I work as a security guard for Nita First

3   National Bank. My brother is a gunsmith. He has a gun shop way on the south side of town.

4

5   I understand that J.J. O'Neill is charged with the murder of his wife, Liza, on the night of

6   September 10, YR-1, and that they say he shot her while she was standing on the porch there.

7   I was at home that night, and I didn't see Liza O'Neill get shot.

8

9   J.J. O'Neill has been one of my brother's customers for many years. I first met him at the

10   shop—my brother introduced us because I'm an avid gamer, and he knew J.J. was also into

11   video games. J.J. now lives up on Northgate Way, but he used to live with his wife in an

12   apartment on Valley Street. At the time she was shot they had separated. She had left him

13   and gone back to live with her stepmother on Prospect Street, and he had gone back to live

14   at the house on Northgate where he had lived before he and Liza got married in YR-2. I know

15   J.J. pretty well. We're both members of "The Guild," a club for gamers here in Nita City, and

16   we often hang out together.

17

18   Yes, I saw J.J. on the night of September 10, YR-1. At about 9:30 or 9:35 p.m. that night he

19   came to our house. I was alone there; my brother had gone out. I cannot fix the exact time

20   J.J. came over, but my best recollection is that it was about 9:30 to 9:35. We talked together

21   for a few minutes, and I guess he was there for about ten minutes or so. I cannot give you the

22   exact time, but I went to bed at 10:00 p.m.—I looked at the clock when I set my alarm. He had

23   been gone about fifteen to twenty minutes before I turned in. I remember brushing my teeth,

24   taking out the trash, and changing clothes, so it had to be fifteen or twenty minutes before *9:35-*

25   10:00 p.m. when he left. There was nothing special about that night, other than seeing J.J. *9:45*

26

27   Yes, we talked when he came over that night. He asked if his gun was ready—he had left his

28   Glock 17 with me to give to my brother for repair and cleaning about a week before. I gave him

29   his gun, and he paid the bill. When I handed the gun to him, I saw him look at it and remove

30   the magazine. I noticed that it had two bullets in the magazine. They must have been in it when

31   he left it with my brother for repair and cleaning. I remember I said to him that he'd better be

32   careful because it was loaded, or something like that. I was surprised—my brother must have

33   removed the magazine when he was cleaning the gun and then replaced it, but never said

34   anything to me about the bullets. J.J. did not remove them when I gave him the gun. He put the

35   gun in his jacket pocket. The jacket was dark blue or black in color, sort of wet, as if he had worn

36   it out in the rain that night. It had been raining off and on all evening. I didn't notice anything

37   weird about his manner or his appearance. He seemed quite calm, not nervous or agitated.

38

39   When he left, I went to the door and looked out the window. It was raining and dark; there

40   was no moonlight. I saw him walk from our front door down the walk to the curb in front of

41   our house and get in a car that was parked there at the curb. It was so dark and rainy that

1   I could not see what kind of car he had. I had seen him on other occasions drive up in an older,
2   black Honda Civic, but this time when I looked out it was so dark and rainy that I could not tell
3   what kind of car it was. I couldn't even make out the color of the car. All I could see out there
4   at the curb was the dark outline or shadow of the car he got into.
5
6   After he got into the car, I could not make out his face or features. The distance from the front
7   door of our house out to the curb is thirty-five feet—I've measured it myself—it was too dark
8   for me to see his face or features. Of course, from having been talking to him in the house,
9   I knew it was J.J. O'Neill. But with the darkness, the rain, and the distance, you would need
10 cat's eyes to see the man in the car at the curb. I don't have that kind of eyesight; nobody does.
11
12 Even though I knew from previous experience that he usually drove an old Honda Civic, I could
13 not swear that he had the same car that night. I can swear that, as I looked out the window
14 to the curb that night, I could not see what kind of car he had, nor even make out the color of
15 it. It was too dark, and the distance was too great.
16
17 **J.J.'S REPUTATION**
18
19 I belong to a group in Nita City called "The Guild," and J.J. is also a member. It's basically a
20 kind of social club for really serious gamers, and we meet every couple of weeks. As far as
21 I know, everyone in the club really likes J.J. I've definitely heard people talk about what a
22 skilled gamer he is. We've mostly talked about games we play, but he's also shared some of
23 his game design concepts with us. They sound pretty sweet, but I don't know that he's ever
24 made any money off of the ideas. I'm definitely more into game playing than design, so I don't
25 really know how likely it is that his business is going to take off or anything. I do know that
26 when I first met J.J. in YR-4, he was working at a computer store and spending basically all of
27 his spare time doing what he described as research and development for his gaming business.
28
29 From all the conversations I had with the members of the group about J.J. O'Neill, I would
30 say he had a reputation for honesty and decency. He's known as being a pretty quiet guy, and
31 definitely really chill, too—not one of those silent rage types, if you know what I mean.
32
33 I heard from other members of the group that in July, YR-1, he and his wife got into it, and
34 that she went back to her stepmother's place just down the street from here. J.J. moved back
35 in with his buddy's sister. Rumor was that Liza had left him, and he was pretty down about it.
36 I'd only met her a couple of times myself, but I know that the mother-in-law was a real piece
37 of work and that she thought J.J.'s business was stupid. She was married to Judge Wilson and
38 all and was a real fancy kind of lady. From what I know, the separation wasn't J.J.'s fault at all,
39 and it was actually entirely the mother-in-law's doing. In any case, Mrs. Wilson wasn't Liza's
40 real mother, but was her stepmother.
41
42 I definitely think of J.J. as being an honest and decent guy. As far as I know, my brother never
43 had any billing problems with him. I would certainly believe anything he said, even if he
44 weren't under oath. From my own knowledge of him and from the reputation he had among
45 the other members of our group, I would say that he was not the kind of guy who would hurt

avid gamer?

Not used to close eyesight

1   anybody, and definitely not his wife. I never saw him lose his temper. I never heard about any
2   such thing either.
3
4   I don't think he killed his wife. He is a victim of circumstance and of a mistaken identification
5   made by Mrs. Wilson, the stepmother. I understand she claims she saw him fire the gun that
6   night out at the curb in front of her house in the dark with no lights, while it was raining. The
7   whole thing is nuts. I think she just hated J.J. so much that she wants to believe that he's Liza's
8   murderer. She saw what she wanted to see.
9
10   I'll tell you who I think might have done it. I used to work as a bailiff for old Judge Wilson,
11   Liza's father. He sent a lot of guys away for a long time, and some of them wanted to get
12   even. There was this one fellow, John Bierman, who thought Judge Wilson had ruined his life
13   and Bierman threatened to get him for it. In 1993, Bierman was convicted of murdering his
14   business partner, who was very well-known in town—witnesses at the trial said Bierman had
15   some kind of Mob connections. It was all over the news at the time. Bierman claimed the
16   judge and the prosecutor rigged the trial. Bierman's whole life was wrecked; he lost a good
17   business, his family, everything, and got twenty to thirty years from Judge Wilson.
18
19   Last summer I read in the newspaper that Bierman was getting out of prison and was returning
20   to Nita City. In early September of last year, I saw Bierman at the Deluxe Bar and Grille.
21   I recognized him right away, even though the trial was almost twenty years ago, because he
22   had a very distinctive face, and he hadn't changed much. I was sitting at the bar fairly close
23   to Bierman, but I'm sure he didn't recognize me. I heard him tell the bartender that the judge
24   had railroaded him. He said he was glad Wilson was dead, but that it didn't even come close
25   to making up for everything he had lost: his family, his business, everything.
26
27   I haven't seen Bierman since that night, but I know J.J. O'Neill, and I don't believe he could
28   have done this. I think the police should track down this Bierman guy.
29
30   It is true that on a number of occasions J.J. O'Neill bragged that he was an excellent shot. He
31   said that he practiced target shooting regularly. I remember once he told me that he could hit
32   a dime at 100 yards, although I know that's impossible, at least with a handgun.
                 Says he knows him, but isn't very close with him
33
34   J.J. rarely discussed his personal life with me, and I didn't know much about his problems with
35   Liza or his mother-in-law. I mostly heard about that stuff from other members of "The Guild."

I have read the above statement and it is true and correct.

Name: *Sam Russo*

Date: October 16, YR-1

Witness: Jack Peters

Date: October 16, YR-1

WARNING AND WAIVER

WARNING AS TO RIGHTS

CASE NO. <u>275622</u>

Before we ask you any questions, it is our duty as police officers to advise you of your rights and to warn you of the consequences of waiving your rights.

You have the absolute right to remain silent.

Anything you say to us can be used against you in court.

You have the right to talk to an attorney before answering any questions and to have an attorney present with you during questioning.

You have this same right to the advice and presence of an attorney, whether you can afford to hire one or not. We have no way of furnishing you with an attorney, but one will be appointed for you, if you wish.

If you decide to answer questions now without an attorney present, you will still have the right to stop answering at any time. You also have the right to stop answering at any time until you talk to an attorney.

WAIVER

I have read the above statement of my rights, and it has been read to me. I understand what my rights are. I wish to make a voluntary statement, and I do not want an attorney. No force, threats, or promises of any kind or nature have been used by anyone in any way to influence me to waive my rights. I am signing this statement after having been advised of my rights, before any questions have been asked of me by the police.

Joe O'Neill
(Signature)

CERTIFICATION

I hereby certify that the foregoing warning and waiver were read by me to the person who has affixed his signature above, and that he also read it and signed it in my presence this <u>10th</u> day of <u>September, YR-1</u>, at <u>11:25</u> o'clock <u>p.m.</u> at <u>Police Headquarters,</u> Nita City.

<u>Allen J. Bradley</u>
(Signature - Police Officer)

Allen J. Bradley, Det.

Frank Novak
(Witness)

Officer Frank Novak

VOLUNTARY STATEMENT

Case #: <u>275622</u>

DATE: <u>September 10, YR-1</u>   PLACE: <u>Police Headquarters,</u>
                                                        <u>Nita City, Nita</u>

Time Statement Started: _____ a.m. <u>11:25</u> p.m.

I, the undersigned, <u>Joseph J. O'Neill</u> of <u>1262 Northgate Way, Nita City, Nita</u> being <u>30</u> years of age, born at <u>Nita City, Nita</u> on <u>June 11, YR-30,</u> do hereby make the following statement to <u>Allen J. Bradley,</u> he having first identified himself as a <u>Detective with the Nita City Police Department</u>.

This statement is voluntarily made by me without any threats, coercion, or promises of any kind or nature. Before making any statement to the police, I was advised that I had the absolute right to remain silent and that anything I might say could be used against me in a criminal proceeding. I was advised also of my right to have an attorney present before answering any questions and that, if I was unable to afford one, an attorney would be provided before questioning. I have freely and voluntarily waived my right to remain silent and my right to consult with an attorney before answering questions.

Q.   Have you had your rights read to you?

A.   YES

Q.   Do you understand your rights?

A.   YES

Whereupon Mr. O'Neill gave the following statement:

I don't know anything about my wife, Liza, being shot. I had nothing to do with the murder. I wasn't even near her stepmother's house at the time of the shooting. I had stopped to see Liza earlier that night around 7:00 or 7:30 p.m., but she had gone to a movie. I stopped at the Harvard Exit Theater, but I didn't see her. I had a couple of drinks at the Deluxe Bar and Grille and then decided to go home. I thought I would see Liza tomorrow.

VOLUNTARY STATEMENT

Case #: <u>275622</u>

DATE: <u>September 10, YR-1</u>　　　　PLACE:　　　<u>Police Headquarters,</u>
　　　　　　　　　　　　　　　　　　　　　　　<u>Nita City, Nita</u>

<u>Page Two</u>

On the way home, I stopped at Sam Russo's house on Prospect between 19th and 20th. I picked up the gun I use for target practice. I had left it with him to be cleaned. That is the gun Officer Novak saw in my room and brought here with him. After I picked up the gun, I went straight home. You can check this out with Mr. Sam Russo. I'm also pretty sure that Amber Donovan heard me come in. I wasn't near 1704 East Prospect Street at 10:00 p.m., and I certainly didn't shoot my wife. I loved her. I picked up the gun from Russo and went straight home to my place on Northgate. The gun you have wasn't fired after I picked it up from Russo.

I have read this statement consisting of <u>2</u> page(s) and the facts contained therein are true and correct.

WITNESSES:

<u>Allen J. Bradley</u>

Allen J. Bradley, Det.

<u>Joe O'Neill</u>

Signature of Person giving

voluntary statement

<u>Frank Novak</u>

Officer Frank Novak

TIME STATEMENT FINISHED: _____ a.m. <u>11:40</u> p.m.

DATE: <u>September 10, YR-1</u>

JOHN PIERCE

John Pierce is a sergeant with the Nita City Police Department. Sergeant Pierce is presently in charge of the Nita City Police Department Crime Lab. He has been working in the Crime Lab for seventeen years, serving as its head for the last five. Sergeant Pierce is a firearms expert and has been qualified as such in court on several occasions.

Sergeant Pierce filed a report on his examination of the Glock 17 recovered from Joseph J. O'Neill's apartment at 1262 Northgate Way and the 9 mm slug recovered at the scene, 1704 East Prospect Street.

Sergeant Pierce has had years of experience with the assembly, disassembly, and cleaning of firearms.

Sergeant Pierce will testify to the following with respect to the cleaning of a handgun:

1. That the time required to thoroughly clean a handgun depends on the number of times the weapon has been fired, and also, to some extent, the particular type of handgun.

2. That a Glock 17 is not a difficult semiautomatic handgun to clean.

3. That a 9 mm semiautomatic handgun like O'Neill's that is quite dirty (substantial powder residue from a number of firings) can be thoroughly cleaned in thirty to forty-five minutes.

4. That a 9 mm semiautomatic handgun that is moderately dirty can be thoroughly cleaned in twenty to thirty minutes.

5. That a 9 mm semiautomatic handgun that has been fired less than ten times after a thorough cleaning can be cleaned in ten minutes or less.

6. That a 9 mm semiautomatic handgun that has been fired once or twice after a thorough cleaning can be cleaned in five minutes or less.

NITA CITY POLICE DEPARTMENT
CRIME LAB REPORT

Lab File No.:   4011

RE: Gunshot residue test, ballistics test, and examination of Glock 17

Case: Liza O'Neill Homicide

Date of Report: September 11, YR-1

Submitted By: Sergeant John Pierce

On September 11, YR-1, I was requested by Detective Allen J. Bradley of the Homicide Division to conduct an analysis of the evidence recovered in the O'Neill homicide. At approximately 8:50 a.m., I obtained a 9 mm handgun (Glock 17) and a 9 mm slug from the Custodian's Office for analysis. These items were recovered by Officer Frank Novak and his initials appeared thereon. I also obtained the Crime Lab Report prepared by Technician Thomas Weibel on the gunshot residue test administered to Joseph J. O'Neill on September 10, YR-1.

Gunshot Residue Test

Technician Weibel administered a gunshot residue test on the defendant, Joseph J. O'Neill, at approximately 12:00 a.m., September 10, YR-1. Technician Weibel's analysis of the test results indicated that the test was negative.

I examined the test data and my findings concur with that of Technician Weibel. The test was negative for the firing of a gun.

The negative finding can mean any one of several things:

    (a) The individual did not fire a gun;

    (b) The individual did fire a gun, but no detectable residue particles were left on the individual's hand for any one of several reasons, such as:

        (1) The individual was wearing gloves; or

        (2) The individual cleaned his or her hands.

Ballistics Test

The Glock 17 was test-fired. It is operable. The test-fired slug was obtained, and comparison was attempted with the slug found at the scene. No comparison could be made, as the slug found at the scene was too deformed to obtain any points of comparison.

Examination of the slug found at the scene indicates it is a 9 mm bullet.

Examination of 9 mm handgun (Glock 17)

Visual (including microscopic) examination and physical tests were performed on the gun recovered from Joseph J. O'Neill.

Examination and tests revealed:

(1) The gun was remarkably clean.

(2) There were traces of oil in the mechanism.

(3) It had been recently exposed to water.

The examination revealed no powder residue or stains. The traces of oil found in the mechanism and the absence of a buildup of powder residue clearly indicate a recent thorough cleaning. Examination also revealed traces of water in the mechanism, and Officer Novak's report indicated that the gun was wet when recovered.

Conclusion

The gun had been recently cleaned. No evidence of firing since the last cleaning was detected.

Submitted By:

John Pierce

John Pierce Badge #674

NITA COUNTY CORONER

STATE OF NITA   )

)   SS:

COUNTY OF NITA   )

I, <u>Elizabeth Martin, MD</u>, Coroner of said County, having examined the body of <u>Liza Wilson O'Neill</u> at <u>Norwegian Medical Center, September 10, YR-1</u>, same having there and then been identified in my presence by <u>Mrs. Mary Wilson</u> as the body of <u>her stepdaughter, Liza Wilson O'Neill,</u> do hereby find that said <u>Liza Wilson O'Neill</u>, deceased, died as a result of a gunshot wound. Said deceased being a <u>female</u> of the age of <u>26</u> years; weight <u>112 lbs.</u>; height <u>5 ft. 6 in.</u>; hair <u>blond</u>; eyes <u>blue</u>; complexion <u>fair</u>; race <u>Caucasian</u>.

REMARKS: Decedent brought to hospital in ambulance at about 10:35 p.m., September 10, YR-1. Decedent DOA. Examination of body disclosed bullet wound from firearm—bullet entered upper chest in front, in area of heart, and was ejected from body in back. Massive hemorrhages resulted, causing death. No powder burns, no physical deformities found on examination. Firearm apparently discharged at some distance from body of deceased. No autopsy. Bullet likely discharged from handgun of some kind.

                                In testimony whereof I have hereunto set my hand and seal of my office this <u>11</u>th day of <u>September</u>, YR-1.

SEAL

Office of
County Coroner
NITA COUNTY
Nita

                                Elizabeth Martin, M.D.
                                Coroner of NITA COUNTY

                                State of Nita

Exhibit 1

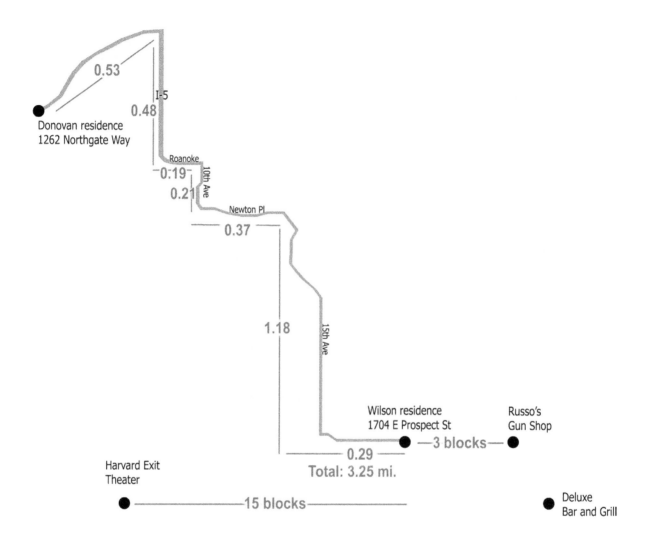

Exhibit 2

OFFICE OF THE CITY ENGINEER
NITA CITY, NITA

I, Ray Hoffman, hereby certify that:

1.   I am Deputy City Engineer of Nita City, Nita, and in that capacity have custody and control of all maps, diagrams, charts, and documents filed in the City Engineer's Office.

2.   On October 13, YR-1, I made the attached copy of the original map of Section 100 of Nita City, Nita, as prepared by N. Allen Crow and filed in City Engineer's Office on September 25, YR-2.

3.   The attached copy of the original map was made by utilizing a standard photocopying machine in the City Engineer's Office. The scale upon which the original map was drawn, as indicated thereon, is correctly shown on the attached copy in feet. I have examined the attached copy and found it to be a correct and accurate representation of the original map.

4.   Since the filing of the above-mentioned map on September 25, YR-2, no amendments with respect to that map have been filed in the City Engineer's Office.

5.   At the request of the District Attorney's Office of Nita County, Nita, I have indicated on the attached copy the following data as ascertained by me from records on file in the City Engineer's Office:

"A" = Residence of Mrs. Mary Wilson (north side of East Prospect Street);

"B" = Harvard Exit Theater (south side of Roy Street);

"C" = Deluxe Bar and Grill (south side of Roy Street);

"D" = Residence of Sam Russo (north side of East Prospect Street);

"E" = Home of Ms. Amber Donovan (northwest side of Northgate Way).

Dated: October 13, YR-1

Ray Hoffman
Deputy City Engineer
Nita City, Nita

I, Mary L. Johnson, Clerk of the Circuit Court, Nita County, Nita City, Nita, do hereby certify that Ray Hoffman is a Deputy City Engineer and that he signed the above document in my presence.

Mary L. Johnson   Mary L. Johnson, Clerk

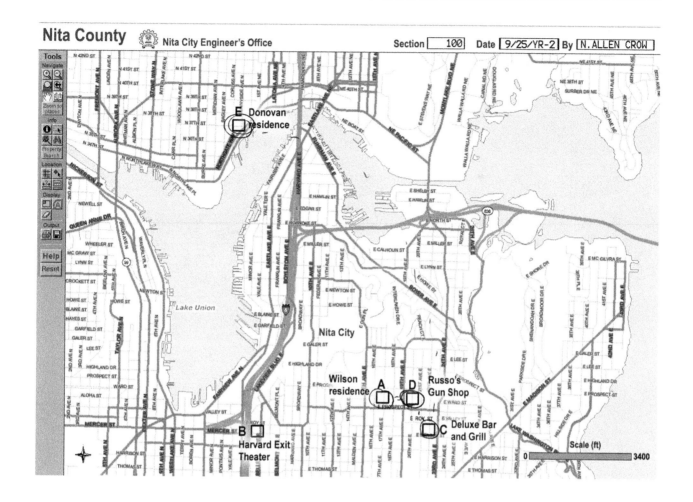

9:30pm

Exhibit 3

Exhibit 4

Exhibit 5

Exhibit 6

Exhibit 7

1704 E Prospect

NITA CITY PD CSI 11:30 NOVV11 YR-1

Exhibit 8

1704 E Prospect

NITA CITY PD CSI 11:31:42 NOV11 YR-1

Exhibit 9

1704 E Prospect

NITA CITY PD CSI 11:33:12 NOV11 YR-1

Exhibit 10

1704 E Prospect

NITA CITY PD CSI 11:37:22 NOV11 YR-1

Exhibit 11

1704 E Prospect

NITA CITY PD CSI 11:37:22 NOV11 YR-1

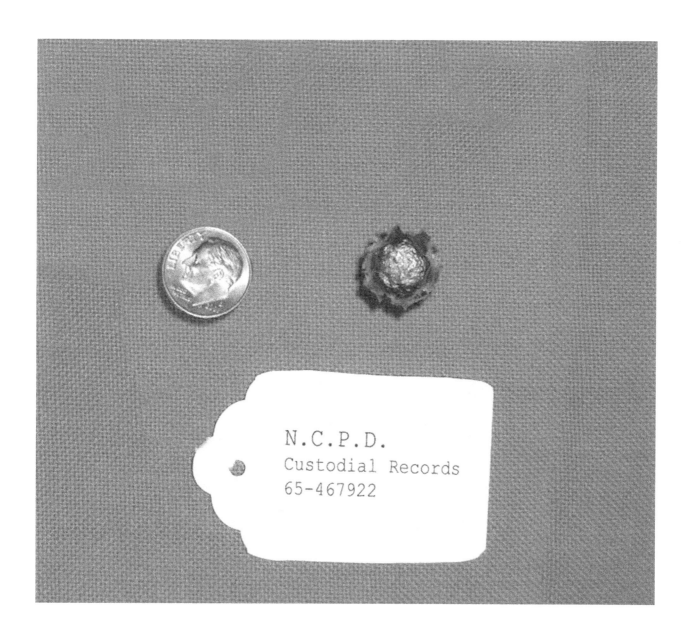

Exhibit 14

NITA CITY POLICE DEPT

<u>PROPERTY INVENTORY</u>

Owner's Name: Joseph O'Neill
Address: 1262 Northgate Way.   Nita City, Nita 45467

ITEM	ITEM TYPE	BRAND/ MAKE	MODEL	SIZE/ COLOR	SERAIL #	ENGRAVINGS/ MARKINGS	OTHER
Pistol	Semi- auto	Glock	17	Black	68717678		
FURTHER DESCRIPTION:	Recovered at O'Neill's Apt..1262 Northgate Way, Nita City						
Bullet	Fired	9mm	9mm				
FURTHER DESCRIPTION:	Recovered at O'Neill's Apt..1262 Northgate Way, Nita City						
Jacket	Long- sleeved	UNKWN		Dark			
FURTHER DESCRIPTION:	Recovered at O'Neill's Apt..1262 Northgate Way, Nita City						
FURTHER DESCRIPTION:							
FURTHER DESCRIPTION:							

Inventory Officer(s): *Frank Novak*   Time (24Hr):

Received y: *Jon M. Grah*   Time (24Hr):

Received by *John Puire*   Crime lab items #1 & 3   Time (24Hr): 08:50
                                                                    9-11-YR1

Received by: *Thomas Jackson*   Time (24Hr):
            Clerk, Custodian Officer items 1+3   450 am 9-11-YR1

Received by: Time (24Hr):

Received by: Time (24Hr):

Exhibit 15

Exhibit 16

Exhibit 17

Exhibit 18

Tsunami Entertainment
1545 Gleason Ave NW Ste 500
San Francisco, CA 94309
(425) 546-7777

BayBank®

No. 2345

6-45983

Date 9/2/YR-1

Pay To The
Order Of   Joseph J. O'Neil $ 2,500

Two thousand five hundred dollars 00/100

Memo: Advance

⑈00000 1004⑈ ⑆1 2 3 4 5 6 7 8 9⑆0 1 2 3 4 5 6 7 8 9⑈

Exhibit 19

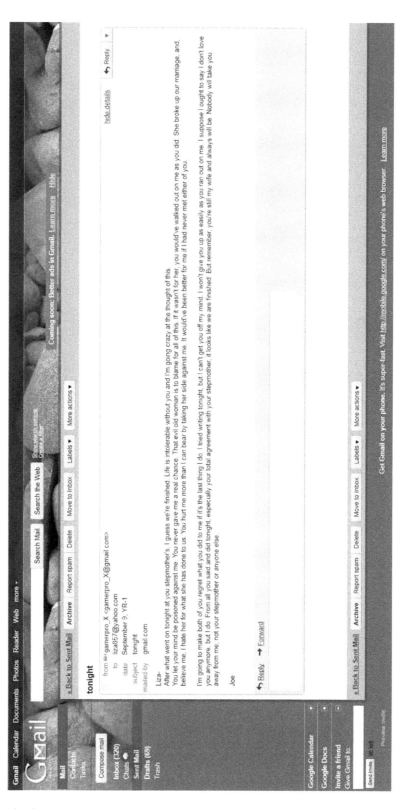

Exhibit 20

THIS IS AN IMPORTANT RECORD
SAFEGUARD IT.

PERSONAL DATA	1. LAST NAME-FIRST NAME-MIDDLE NAME JOSEPH J. ONEIL	2. SERVICE NUMBER	3. SOCIAL SECURITY NUMBER 543 | 33 | 3421

4. DEPARTMENT, COMPONENT AND BRANCH OR CLASS	5a. GRADE, RATE OR RANK	b. PAY GRADE	6. DATE OF RANK
ARMY RA SIG	SP4	E-4	DAY 29 / MONTH OCT / YEAR YR-12

7. U.S. CITIZEN	8. PLACE OF BIRTH (City and State or County)	9. DATE OF BIRTH
☒ YES ☐ NO	TEXAS	DAY 11 / MONTH JUN / YEAR YR-30

SELECTIVE SERVICE DATA

10a. SELECTIVE SERVICE NUMBER	b. SELECTIVE SERVICE LOCAL BOARD NUMBER, CITY, COUNTY, STATE AND ZIP CODE	c. DATE INDUCTED
		DAY / MONTH / YEAR NA

TRANSFER OR DISCHARGE DATA

11a. TYPE OF TRANSFER OR DISCHARGE TRF	b. STATION OR INSTALLATION AT WHICH EFFECTED FT DIX NJ	
c. REASON AND AUTHORITY AR 635-200 SPN 411 EARLY SEP FR		d. EFFECTIVE DATE DAY 31 / MONTH MAR / YEAR YR-8

12. LAST DUTY ASSIGNMENT AND MAJOR COMMAND SVC BTRY 2D BN 6TH ARTY	13a. CHARACTER OF SERVICE GENERAL	b. TYPE OF CERTIFICATE ISSUED NONE

14. DISTRICT, AREA COMMAND OR CORPS TO WHICH RESERVIST TRANSFERRED TRF AR CON GP (REINF) USAAC ST LOUIS MO	15. REENLISTMENT CODE RE-1

16. TERMINAL DATE OF RESERVE/UMT&S OBLIGATION	17. CURRENT ACTIVE SERVICE OTHER THAN BY INDUCTION		18. TERM OF SERVICE	c. DATE OF ENTRY
DAY / MONTH / YEAR	a. SOURCE OF ENTRY: ☒ ENLISTED (First Enlistment) ☐ ENLISTED (Prior Service) ☐ REENLISTED ☐ OTHER		a. (Years)	DAY / MONTH / YEAR

18. PRIOR REGULAR ENLISTMENTS NONE	19. GRADE, RATE OR RANK AT TIME OF ENTRY INTO CURRENT ACTIVE SVC PV-1	20. PLACE OF ENTRY INTO CURRENT ACTIVE SERVICE (City and State) SPOKANE WASHINGTON

SERVICE DATA

21. HOME OF RECORD AT TIME OF ENTRY INTO ACTIVE SERVICE (Street, RFD, City, County, State and ZIP Code)	22. STATEMENT OF SERVICE		YEARS	MONTHS	DAYS
	a. CREDITABLE FOR BASIC PAY PURPOSES	(1) NET SERVICE THIS PERIOD	3	11	20
		(2) OTHER SERVICE	0	0	0
23a. SPECIALTY NUMBER & TITLE 36K20 WIREMAN	b. RELATED CIVILIAN OCCUPATION AND D.O.T. NUMBER 829.281 WIREMAN MAINT	(3) TOTAL (Line (1) plus Line (2))	3	11	20
		b. TOTAL ACTIVE SERVICE	3	11	20
		c. FOREIGN AND/OR SEA SERVICE SEE 30	1	9	26

24. DECORATIONS, MEDALS, BADGES, COMMENDATIONS, CITATIONS AND CAMPAIGN RIBBONS AWARDED OR AUTHORIZED

25. EDUCATION AND TRAINING COMPLETED
ATP 21-114
CODE OF COND
C B R TNG
RVN TNG
WIREMAN   8 WKS 67

VA AND EMP SERVICE DATA

26a. NON-PAY PERIODS TIME LOST (Preceding Two Years) NA	b. DAYS ACCRUED LEAVE PAID NA	27a. INSURANCE IN FORCE (NSLI or USGLI) ☐ YES ☒ NO	b. AMOUNT OF ALLOTMENT NA	c. MONTH ALLOTMENT DISCONTINUED NA
	28. VA CLAIM NUMBER c. NA	29. SERVICEMEN'S GROUP LIFE INSURANCE COVERAGE ☒ $10,000 ☐ $5,000 ☐ NONE		

REMARKS

30. REMARKS
BLOOD GP O
8 YRS ELEM (GEN)
USARPAC VIETNAM 22 OCT   - 20 OCT
USAREUR GERMANY 3 JUN   - 5 APR

AUTHENTICATION

31. PERMANENT ADDRESS FOR MAILING PURPOSES AFTER TRANSFER OR DISCHARGE (Street, RFD, City, County, State and ZIP Code)	32. SIGNATURE OF PERSON BEING TRANSFERRED OR DISCHARGED *Joseph Oneil*
33. TYPED NAME, GRADE AND TITLE OF AUTHORIZING OFFICER CPT FA ASST CHIEF ENL BRANCH	34. SIGNATURE OF OFFICER AUTHORIZED TO SIGN

DD FORM 214
1 JUL 66

PREVIOUS EDITIONS OF THIS FORM ARE OBSOLETE EFFECTIVE 1 JAN 67

☆ GPO: 1969-351-112

ARMED FORCES OF THE UNITED STATES
REPORT OF TRANSFER OR DISCHARGE

2

Exhibit 21

Auto sales statistics and black model examples, year YR-12

Toyota Camry -4th best selling passenger vehicle in the US   422,961

Honda Accord -5th best selling passenger vehicle in the US   404,515

Ford Taurus   -6th best selling passenger vehicle in the US   382,035

Honda Civic   -7th best selling passenger vehicle in the US   324,528

Nissan Maxima   109,345

Exhibit 22

Nita City Daily Ne

*ty Guide Section B - **Weather** Section D - **Sports** Section E - **Business** Section A -*

Local Businessman Sentenced in Murd

ilie
the
pri-
im
tly.

l be
liff-
c of
and
me
ong
ith-

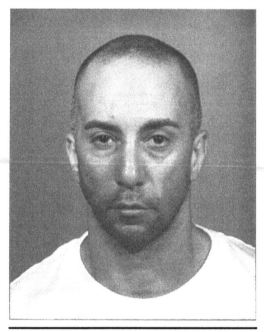

John Bierman

Nita City businessman John Bierman was sentenced today for the murder of his business partner Adam Scherring. Bierman had accused Judge Harry Wilson and the prosecutor of framing him for the murder.

Earlier, the jury convicted Bierman after only two hours of deliberation. Judge Wilson sentenced Bierman to 30 years in Nita State Prison for the murder convinced by the prosecution to use maximum sentencing guidelines becau of Bierman's history with organized cri crime in Nita City and Nita Valley Tow

Applicable Nita Statutes

Nita Criminal Code - Chapter 40.

Section 18-3-101. Homicide - definition of terms.

(1) "Homicide" means the killing of a person by another.

(2) "Person," when referring to the victim of a homicide, means a human being who had been born and was alive at the time of the homicidal act.

(3) The term "after deliberation" means not only intentionally, but also that the decision to commit the act has been made after the exercise of reflection and judgment concerning the act. An act committed after deliberation is never one which has been committed in a hasty or impulsive manner.

Section 18-3-102. Murder in the first degree.

(1) A person commits the crime of murder in the first degree if:

After deliberation and with the intent to cause the death of a person, other than himself or herself, he or she causes the death of that person or of another person.

(2) Murder in the first degree is a class 1 felony.

Section 18-3-103. Murder in the second degree.

(1) A person commits the crime of murder in the second degree if:

(a) He or she intentionally, but not after deliberation, causes the death of a person; or

(b) With intent to cause serious bodily injury to a person other than himself or herself, he or she causes the death of that person or of another person.

(2) Diminished responsibility due to lack of mental capacity is not a defense to murder in the second degree.

(3) Murder in the second degree is a class 2 felony.

Section 18-1-105. Felonies classified; penalties.

Felonies are divided into classes, which are distinguished from one another by the following penalties which are authorized upon conviction:

Class	Minimum Sentence	Maximum Sentence
1	Fifty years imprisonment	Life imprisonment
2	Ten years imprisonment	Fifty years imprisonment

* * *

Section 18-1-501. Principles of Criminal Culpability. Definitions.

The following definitions are applicable to the determination of culpability requirements for offenses defined in this code:

(1) "Act" means a bodily movement, and includes words and possession of property.

(2) "Conduct" means an act or omission and its accompanying state of mind, or, where relevant, a series of acts or omissions.

* * *

(5) "Intentionally." A person acts intentionally with respect to a result or to conduct described by a statute defining an offense when his or her conscious objective is to cause such result or to engage in such conduct.

(6) "Knowingly." A person acts knowingly with respect to conduct or to a circumstance described by a statute defining an offense when he or she is aware that his or her conduct is of such nature or that such circumstance exists.

---

*These proposed instructions are those applicable to this case only. They are borrowed or adapted from Colorado, Indiana, and Illinois Pattern Jury Instructions.

Proposed Jury Instructions*

1.   The Court will now instruct you on the law governing this case. You must arrive at your verdict by unanimous vote, applying the law, as you are now instructed, to the facts as you find them to be.

2.   The State of Nita has charged the defendant, Joseph J. O'Neill, with the crime of First Degree Murder, which includes the crime of Second Degree Murder. The defendant has pleaded Not Guilty.

3.   Under the criminal code of the State of Nita, a person commits the crime of First Degree Murder if, after deliberation and with the intent to cause the death of a person, other than himself or herself, he or she causes the death of that person or of another person.

"Person," when referring to the victim of a homicide, means a human being who had been born and was alive at the time of the homicidal act.

"After deliberation" means not only intentionally, but also that the decision to commit the act has been made after the exercise of reflection and judgment concerning the act. An act committed after deliberation is never one which has been committed in a hasty or impulsive manner.

4.   Under the criminal code of the State of Nita, a person commits the crime of Second Degree Murder if:

    (a)   He or she intentionally, but not after deliberation, causes the death of a person; or

    (b)   With intent to cause serious bodily injury to a person, other than himself or herself, he or she causes the death of that person or of another person.

        "Intentionally." A person acts intentionally with respect to a result or to conduct described by a statute defining a crime when his or her conscious objective is to cause such result or to engage in such conduct.

5.   To sustain the charge of First Degree Murder, the State must prove the following propositions:

    (a)   That defendant performed the acts which caused the death of Liza Wilson O'Neill, a human being; and

    (b)   That defendant acted after deliberation and with the intent to cause the death of Liza Wilson O'Neill or any other person. —> at The bar

        If you find from your consideration of all the evidence that each of these propositions has been proved beyond a reasonable doubt, then you should find the defendant guilty of First Degree Murder.

        If, on the other hand, you find from your consideration of all the evidence that any of these propositions has not been proved beyond a reasonable doubt, then you should find the defendant not guilty of First Degree Murder.

6.   To sustain the charge of Second Degree Murder, the State must prove the following propositions:

    (a)   That defendant performed the acts which caused the death of Liza Wilson O'Neill, a human being; and

(b) That defendant intended to kill or cause serious bodily injury to Liza Wilson O'Neill or any other person.

If you find from your consideration of all the evidence that each of these propositions has been proved beyond a reasonable doubt, then you should find the defendant guilty of Second Degree Murder.

If on the other hand, you find from your consideration of all the evidence that any of these propositions has not been proved beyond a reasonable doubt, then you should find the defendant not guilty of Second Degree Murder.

---

* The instructions contained in this section are borrowed or adapted from a number of sources including California, Illinois, Indiana, Washington, and Colorado pattern jury instructions.

Nita
General Jury Instructions

The following jury instructions are intended for use with any of the files contained in these materials regardless of whether the trial is in Nita State Court or in Federal Court. In addition, each of the files contains special instructions on dealing with the law applicable in the particular case. The instructions set forth here state general principles that may be applicable in any of the cases and may be used at the discretion of the trial judge.*

PART I
PRELIMINARY INSTRUCTIONS GIVEN PRIOR TO THE EVIDENCE
(For Civil or Criminal Cases)

Nita Instruction 01:01 — Introduction

You have been selected as jurors and have taken an oath to well and truly try this cause. This trial will last one day.

During the progress of the trial there will be periods of time when the Court recesses. During those periods of time, you must not talk about this case among yourselves or with anyone else.

During the trial, do not talk to any of the parties, their lawyers, or any of the witnesses.

If any attempt is made by anyone to talk to you concerning the matters here under consideration, you should immediately report that fact to the Court.

You should keep an open mind. You should not form or express an opinion during the trial and should reach no conclusion in this case until you have heard all of the evidence, the arguments of counsel, and the final instructions as to the law that will be given to you by the Court.

Nita Instruction 01:02 — Conduct of the Trial

First, the attorneys will have an opportunity to make opening statements. These statements are not evidence and should be considered only as a preview of what the attorneys expect the evidence will be.

Following the opening statements, witnesses will be called to testify. They will be placed under oath and questioned by the attorneys. Documents and other tangible exhibits may also be received as evidence. If an exhibit is given to you to examine, you should examine it carefully, individually, and without any comment.

It is counsel's right and duty to object when testimony or other evidence is being offered that he or she believes is not admissible.

When the Court sustains an objection to a question, the jurors must disregard the question and the answer, if one has been given, and draw no inference from the question or answer or speculate as to what the witness would have said if permitted to answer. Jurors must also disregard evidence stricken from the record.

When the Court sustains an objection to any evidence the jurors must disregard that evidence.

When the Court overrules an objection to any evidence, the jurors must not give that evidence any more weight than if the objection had not been made.

When the evidence is completed, the attorneys will make final statements. These final statements are not evidence but are given to assist you in evaluating the evidence. The attorneys are also permitted to argue in an attempt to persuade you to a particular verdict. You may accept or reject those arguments as you see fit.

Finally, just before you retire to consider your verdict, I will give you further instructions on the law that applies to this case.

PART II

FINAL INSTRUCTIONS

GENERAL PRINCIPLES

General Instructions for both Civil and Criminal Cases

Nita Instruction 1:01 — Introduction

Members of the jury, the evidence and arguments in this case have been completed, and I will now instruct you as to the law.

The laws applicable to this case are stated in these instructions and it is your duty to follow all of them. You must not single out certain instructions and disregard others.

It is your duty to determine the facts, and to determine them only from the evidence in this case. You are to apply the law to the facts and in this way decide the case. You must not be governed or influenced by sympathy or prejudice for or against any party in this case. Your verdict must be based on evidence and not upon speculation, guess, or conjecture.

From time to time the Court has ruled on the admissibility of evidence. You must not concern yourselves with the reasons for these rulings. You should disregard questions and exhibits that were withdrawn or to which objections were sustained.

You should also disregard testimony and exhibits that the Court has refused or stricken.

The evidence that you should consider consists only of the witnesses' testimonies and the exhibits the Court has received.

Any evidence that was received for a limited purpose should not be considered by you for any other purpose.

You should consider all the evidence in the light of your own observations and experiences in life.

Neither by these instructions nor by any ruling or remark that I have made do I mean to indicate any opinion as to the facts or as to what your verdict should be.

Nita Instruction 1:02 — Opening Statements and Closing Arguments

Opening statements are made by the attorneys to acquaint you with the facts they expect to prove. Closing arguments are made by the attorneys to discuss the facts and circumstances in the case, and should be confined to the evidence and to reasonable inferences to be drawn therefrom. Neither opening statements nor closing arguments are evidence, and any statement or argument made by the attorneys that is not based on the evidence should be disregarded.

Nita Instruction 1:03 — Credibility of Witnesses

You are the sole judges of the credibility of the witnesses and of the weight to be given to the testimony of each witness. In determining what credit is to be given any witness, you may take into account his or her ability and opportunity to observe; his or her manner and appearance while testifying; any interest, bias, or prejudice he or she may have; the reasonableness of his or her testimony considered in light of all the evidence; and any other factors that bear on the believability and weight of the witness' testimony.

Nita Instruction 1:04 — Expert Witnesses

You have heard evidence in this case from witnesses who testified as experts. The law allows experts to express an opinion on subjects involving their special knowledge, training and skill, experience, or research. While their opinions are allowed to be given, it is entirely within the province of the jury to determine what weight shall be given their testimony. Jurors are not bound by the testimony of experts; their testimony is to be weighed as that of any other witness.

Nita Instruction 1:05 — Direct and Circumstantial Evidence

The law recognizes two kinds of evidence: direct and circumstantial. Direct evidence proves a fact directly; that is, the evidence by itself, if true, establishes the fact. Circumstantial evidence is the proof of facts or circumstances that give rise to a reasonable inference of other facts; that is, circumstantial evidence proves a fact indirectly in that it follows from other facts or circumstances according to common experience and observations in life. An eyewitness is a common example of direct evidence, while human footprints are circumstantial evidence that a person was present.

The law makes no distinction between direct and circumstantial evidence as to the degree or amount of proof required, and each should be considered according to whatever weight or value it may have. All of the evidence should be considered and evaluated by you in arriving at your verdict.

Nita Instruction 1:06 — Concluding Instruction

The Court did not in any way and does not by these instructions give or intimate any opinions as to what has or has not been proven in the case, or as to what are or are not the facts of the case.

No one of these instructions states all of the law applicable, but all of them must be taken, read, and considered together as they are connected with and related to each other as a whole.

You must not be concerned with the wisdom of any rule of law. Regardless of any opinions you may have as to what the law ought to be, it would be a violation of your sworn duty to base a verdict upon any other view of the law than that given in the instructions of the court.

General Instructions for Criminal Cases Only

Nita Instruction 3:01 — Indictment (Information)

The indictment (information) in this case is the formal method of accusing the defendant of a crime and placing him on trial. It is not any evidence against the defendant and does not create any inference of guilt. The (State) (Government) has the burden of proving beyond a reasonable doubt every essential element of the crime charged in the indictment (information) (or any of the crimes included therein).

Nita Instruction 3:02 — Burden of Proof

The (State) (Government) has the burden of proving the guilt of the defendant beyond a reasonable doubt, and this burden remains on the (State) (Government) throughout the case. The defendant is not required to prove his innocence.

Nita Instruction 3:03 — Reasonable Doubt

Reasonable doubt means a doubt based upon reason and common sense that arises from a fair and rational consideration of all the evidence or lack of evidence in the case. It is a doubt that is not a vague, speculative, or imaginary doubt, but such a doubt as would cause reasonable persons to hesitate to act in matters of importance to themselves.

Nita Instruction 3:04 — Presumption of Innocence

The defendant is presumed to be innocent of the charges against him. This presumption remains with him throughout every stage of the trial and during your deliberations on the verdict. The presumption is not overcome until, from all the evidence in the case, you are convinced beyond a reasonable doubt that the defendant is guilty.

Nita Instruction 3:05 — Reputation/Character

The defendant has introduced evidence of his character and reputation for (truth and veracity) (being a peaceful and law-abiding citizen) (morality) (chastity) (honesty and integrity) (etc.). This evidence may be sufficient when considered with the other evidence in the case to raise a reasonable doubt of the defendant's guilt. However, if from all the evidence in the case you are satisfied beyond a reasonable doubt of the defendant's guilt, then it is your duty to find him guilty, even though he may have a good reputation for _____.

IN THE CIRCUIT COURT OF NITA COUNTY, NITA

THE PEOPLE OF THE STATE OF NITA	)	
	)	
v.	)	Case No. CR 2126
	)	
JOSEPH J. O'NEILL	)	JURY VERDICT
	)	
Defendant.	)	

We, the Jury, return the following verdict, and each of us concurs in this verdict:

[Choose the appropriate verdict]

I. NOT GUILTY

We, the Jury, find the defendant, Joseph J. O'Neill, NOT GUILTY.

_____ Foreperson

II. FIRST DEGREE MURDER

We, the Jury, find the defendant, Joseph J. O'Neill, GUILTY of Murder in the First degree.

_____ Foreperson

III. SECOND DEGREE MURDER

We, the Jury, find the defendant, Joseph O'Neill, GUILTY of Murder in the Second Degree.

_____ Foreperson

CPSIA information can be obtained
at www.ICGtesting.com
Printed in the USA
FSHW020144090119

9 781601 562081